In the Country of Birds

JAMES SUTHERLAND-SMITH was born in 1948 in Aberdeen. He is currently working as the Manager for the Peacekeeping English Project in Serbia and Montenegro based in Belgrade. He has published three previous full collections, the last of which, *At the Skin Resort*, appeared in 1999. Together with his wife, Viera, he is the major translator of Slovak poetry into English. Individual book selections of his translations from Ján Búzassy, Mila Haugová, Ivan Laučík, Jozef Leikert and Milan Rúfus have appeared in Canada, Britain and the USA. Book selections of his own work have been published in Slovak and Romanian.

T0149169

JAMES SUTHERLAND-SMITH

In the Country of Birds

CARCANET

First published in Great Britain in 2003 by
Carcanet Press Limited
Alliance House
Cross Street
Manchester M2 7AQ

A CIP catalogue record for this book is available from the British Library
ISBN 1 85754 641 5

The publisher acknowledges financial assistance from
Arts Council England

Typeset in Monotype Bembo by XL Publishing Services, Tiverton
Printed and bound in England by SRP Ltd, Exeter

Contents

Acknowledgements

Eleven of the poems in this collection have appeared in *New Poetries III* (Carcanet, 2002).

'Delays', 'In the Harbour at Leptis Magna', 'Sonnets from Zawia', 'The Country of Rumour', 'The Drowned Boy' appeared in *The Country of Rumour* (Many Press, 1984) and 'A Little Rain in Riyadh', 'English for Special Purposes' and 'Sunrise at the Wadi Nisah' were broadcast in a programme of the same name in the BBC Radio 3 series *The Living Poet* in 1985.

'A Minor Operation' was broadcast on Slovak television's programme on James Sutherland-Smith's work, *Hviezdy a more* ('Stars and Sea') in 1990.

'Customer' is recited by the author on the cassette *Iluzie* (Modry Peter, Slovakia, 1995).

'Grace' appeared in the anthology *The New Exeter Book of Riddles* (Enitharmon, 1999), 'Literacy' and 'The Month of Fasting' in *New Poetry 9* (Hutchinson, 1983), 'A Piece of Wood' in *New Poetry 8* (Hutchinson, 1982)

'A Language Shift' won first prize in the Peterloo Poetry competition in 2002.

'The Country of Birds' won First Prize in the Robert Penn Warren Competition in 2001.

'March Adder' won a prize in the Cardiff International Poetry Competition in 2000.

'South District, Prague' won Second Prize in the Bridport Competition in 1998.

'Belly Dancer Weeping' won Third Prize in the Exeter Poetry Competition in 1997.

'Rainoo Repeats Her English in Bombay' and 'At Huwailah Beach' won the *San Jose Studies* Poetry Award in 1991.

'Ladies of the Bundesrepublik', 'The Drowned Boy', 'The Melon Girl', 'Julie's Recovery' and 'Pariah' were prizewinners in the National Poetry Competition in 1982, 1983, 1986, 1987 and 1989 respectively.

'Translation' and 'The Fossil' were prizewinners in the *TLS/* Cheltenham Festival competition in 1982 and 1986 respectively, with 'A Snail in Istanbul' and 'Rainoo Repeats Her English in Bombay' receiving special mention in 1988. 'Heliopolis' and 'Prickly Pears and Oranges' were also shortlisted in 1986.

'An Execution in Riyadh' won the Phillips Award of *Stone Country Magazine* in 1984.

Poems in this collection have also appeared in the following magazines: *Ambit, Confrontation, Cumberland Poetry Review, Cyphers, Descant, Dog River Review, Encounter, ESP Spectrum* (Slovakia), *Fine Madness, Graham House Review, The Honest Ulsterman, Kansas Quarterly, Laurel Review, Lines, Literary Matters* (British Council), *The Literary Review* (USA), *The North, North Colorado Review, Permafrost, PN Review, Poet Lore, Poetry* (Chicago), *Poetry Durham, Poetry Review, Poetry Wales, Prairie Schooner, Rialto, San Jose Studies, Six Seasons, Stand, West Branch* and *Western Humanities Review*.

Rain Like Lace Curtains

This must be the new candour, houses
Built of raw brick to weather into style,

With lounges see-through to acres of mud,
Double garage doors that lift doubly quiet

By remote control. I raise a dry white wine
In toast at yet another house-warming

Where talk is generous, the husband
In High Tech, the wife in Speech Therapy,

The guests stammering *M-m-money!*
And I watch rain like lace curtains flutter

Between the new estate and cottages
Renovated for those old who live

Just within their means, vote Conservative,
Neglect outside paintwork, rarely entertain.

Beyond them the couple who sold the land
For millions, often argue through the night

Like a gale banging an unlatched door
To let rain gust in along a passage.

They squall obscenely, shock us all.

Scolt Head

From an aerial photograph

Saltmarsh dapple of clay and water:
fritillary; my moods and whims,

inlets bordered with pale sands,
grayling; your discretions,

the sea; my best hours, your eyes, your mercies,
the extinct blues brought back to flourish.

Elsewhere, as far as possible from any ocean,
I've seen them waft down to my bare arm, sip salt.

But now our gaze is shifted higher than the gulls
and can't make out swan necks among rushes,

the butterflies' roller-coasting swoop and soar.
We have been lifted away so far that a world has changed:

the shoreline is a white brush stroke on black paper,
a single touch centuries in execution

or, bent by gale and wave,
it is a ghost departing

or a broken caul where the creeks
outline and vein an embryo.

It is something always dying, never dead
or something always becoming, never born

as tide and weather fret and filter changes.
It is a butterfly antenna dithering

over folded wings of mud and weed
or the curve of a swan's neck about to stretch in flight

or seahorse, no, horsehead nebula of dune and grass,
energy contained and held against absolute zero,

or a place where we could walk and skim flat stones
their splashing lost in the surf's white noise,

a place where we could watch butterflies shilly shally
their serious game of being and non-being.

The Garden of England

It's an afternoon of otters and dragonflies;
One which might be dreamed of by Friends of the Earth
Where recycled paper clothes slip from the shoulders
Of children who don't consume cyclamates.
When they swim they hear in the background
The chug chug of a tractor powered by chicken shit.

I'm thinking of harpsichord music
While the train is tinkling chromatically
Towards Rochester, its noise affable,
Acceptable, accessible under a sky
Weaned from a Gainsborough blue by refineries.
The coastline must be forty rows of pear trees away.

At Gillingham station the feet of passengers mutter
Give us calm apples and the votes of geese.
A voice drains through the tannoy. Soon I'll reach
The estuary where there is a wharf
Owned by a relative's company whose ships
Carry the antiseptic earth used in cat trays.

On Parliament Hill

I should compose a sentence for us
Slender and bare of complication
As a poplar becomes in winter.
It should be singular as a bench on a hill.

It should hint at no more than outlines
Of slopes shaded against searchlights
Which begin to siphon into a sky
Abundant as tidal water.

But this evening the lights of London lie
Like handbooks I do not want to read.
They offer thin paragraphs of tower blocks;
Instructions on how to die without complaint.

Below me a goods train wrangles towards the west
In terminal discourse like a pensioner
Collecting glasses after closing time.
It follows an afternoon which sank away

Into a park I have stayed in too long;
A place of hacked rock slimy with moss
Where flies hang in transistor squadrons.
Far from its vistas you must be driving home

Past a child practising handstands on a green
Or past a man in a striped shirt and braces
Who walks through uncut hay and thinks of nothing
Seeing an express go by to the north.

A Minor Operation

They are like water lily leaves,
These green porcelain disks above me
Which diffuse an even, working light.
I could have walked to the theatre,
But orderlies lifted, wheeled then tipped me
On to a slab; hard black plastic,
Dull as basalt so it can't reflect.
My body casts no shadow in this place.

*You're very lucky. Not many patients
Have come in here fully conscious,*
The surgeon stoops across in a mask
Which has made his face a kind of beak.
I imagine pale green lilies floating
And recall a childhood nature book
Which said *Nothing is more voracious
Than a water beetle in its pond.*

I am here because a growth has inched
Across my skin, across my mind.
I do not think of water lilies now
But of an apple with brown spots
And a worm eating its way through.
Minutes pass until the instruments click
As they drop something into a dish.
The surgeon counts to eight in stitches.

Afterwards I am made to rest
In a ward for Ear, Nose and Throat.
For this is the National Health
Whose lunch I take with Jack and Charlie.
Jack has had both legs amputated
Just below the knee. He does not talk
But props his left thigh on the wheelchair's arm
And swings the stump. He wants home badly.

The air beneath him twitches like a foot
As Charlie, slow multiple sclerosis,
Drones on about the football he once played,
About how he still can catch eel and shrimp
Because the sea supports his weight
While I gaze up for water lilies
And hold an apple whose marvellous skin
My fingers rub as they search for blemish.

Searching For My Father

Jennie kept her fur hat on in Australia House
As we worked our way through the voting lists.
She was very cold. She was an archivist
And had a chum who'd held Napoleon's penis
Before it was auctioned off. Over dinner
The chum said, *It was dried up like a dog turd!*

We eliminated all the Mervs and Mels
To arrive at five suitable Michael Georges;
A soldier, a miner, two company directors
And an agricultural machinery salesman
From Toowoomba, Queensland, my favourite
As my father's letters had said, *Queensland is Paradise!*

That was the best I tried although I wrote to all five
And Petty France who answered, *No record
Of a passport issued to Michael George exists
Since 1959.* No other answers. Jennie left me
For a doctor old enough to be my father.
I hoped his penis was dried up like a dog turd.

In Bombay a sallow astrologer told me,
*When you were eighteen your father left you.
You must treat him as if he were in Paradise,
But you will have an answer soon,* then stood up,
Pressed his hands together and bowed whispering
You have left your money and passport on the chair.

And so in the desert near Durma in Arabia
While visiting four Australian shepherds,
Greg, Phil, Bernie, Theo, I was introduced
To Michael George – *Like a father to us
In this bloody place,* who'd been a salesman
In Toowoomba, Queensland. Had I heard of it?

Somehow they all seemed adult to my child
When I asked if it were an attractive town.
They drew on cigarettes and looked secretive
Like monks listening to an eager novice with questions
On how many angels danced on the head of a pin.
Later we took our shirts off. We were very hot.

Civilisation

I actually saw him once
At a party at the start of a festival.
I was serving drinks.
He'd hennaed his hair.

Mostly the rest was rumour
And songs he'd written
Which a friend read to me
Moving his lips slowly.

They were long-winded celebrations
Of old stones and music and colours
Such as red and blue and green and yellow
Which he called scarlet, azure, emerald, Marie-Thérèse.

There was never the sense of someone hunted
For love or vengeance,
No songs for campfires under starlight,
For cleaning one's gun.

I saw him once again.
I'd heard he'd gone back to work
In a city we'd entered uninvited.
I went to his office, but the door was closed.

I leant my Kalashnikov against the wall
And fiddled with my fake Rolex.
I shouted, *I'm here!*
I want you to teach me how to tell the time!

There was no answer.
I peered through the keyhole.
He was walking up and down stark naked,
Waving his arms, talking to himself.

Rammle

Once he said *Let's clear the garage of this rammle,*
His misspelling the longest lasting of his lies.
I thought the word from Egypt, *ramal* meaning sand
And father being one of Monty's Desert Rats.
But the word's from Sheffield, Nottingham and Derby
And has nowt to do with Alamein or Rommel.
I never guessed that father must have spoken local.
He dropped that with a taste for whisky and a dash of lime
Sniggered at by officers his first day in the mess.
Years later he dropped the desert and just became
A simple rat who bunked off and left his missis
With six young 'uns all of whom spoke public school.

I've looked the word up, spelt rammel in the OED,
Or ramail, ramayle, ramal, ramel, ramelle,
Rammell, rammal, rammale, rammald, ramaille,
Alternatives from Old French meaning branches,
Small, crooked or rubbishy from a tree
Which has been felled, later rubbish of any kind:
1513 Gavin Douglas – Aeneis
    Amang the scroggy rammell settis the fyre
1549 Scotland
    There vas ane grene bancful of rammel grene treis
1616 Nottingham Records
    For clensinge the streets and caryinge away the rammell

1796 Pegge – Derbicisms
—— *rammel – small green spraywood left after the cordwood*
    and all the larger stuff is taken out
1832 – Boston Herald, 6th March
    Some rammel which had been most improperly placed in Broad Street
1870 – E. Peacock's Ralf Skirl
    Tak that rammil back
    I don't want none on it
1894 – Baring-Gould Queen of Love
    The fold was apparently of 'rammel'
    and grew nothing except a little stunted broom
Not forgetting Florio's verb in 1611

> *To rammell or moulder in pieces as sometimes*
> *Mud walles or great masses of stones will do of themselves,*

Much as father must have done of himself.
I've looked at a map of phrases, so many
Overlapping where he was born and raised,
Where the Trent has confluence with the Soar,
Where weather teems or pours into pit or pond
Deep in the heart of where summat might be up,
A she-cat's country of gable-ends and folks not people,
Of gorse not furze, on the borders of dunno and don't,
South of supping ale but north of curse in cussing land,
Well within the forred of the islands' common speeches.

He was born before sideboards emerged from whiskers,
Where coaldust wasn't slack or smallcoal but backing,
Armpit on his western flank, to the east armholes,
Where you do not clean your ears or lugs but tabs, our kid.
Did his Mam shush him when hailstones on the tiles
Rang like horses' hooves not hoofs? Did she tell him
Not to go with poovs or poofs? A neighbour said
He was always hungry or allus clammed (I can't recall
How broad her speech was) because his Dad was mean.
Was he frit or frightened to ax or ask again
For overcoat or topcoat against the backend chill
In case he catched a cold and turned his toes up then?

He got away from dialect right smartish in the war.
Not for him a life of scoffing snap wi' lads at ten.
But thereonafter pissed into the wind so much
He was always wet behind the ears, no bloody use,
A mouth and trousers courting a fur coat
With no knickers on down a ginnel in the rain
Leaving the rest of us all dressed up, nowhere to go
Without so much as Princess Di's hint of glottal stop.
So Dad, wherever you might have buggered off to,
Australia or Canada, Paraguay or hell,
Tha owes it us to have turned tha toes up now
Dead as a dodo, doornail, dead as Latin.

What remains of you are remains: debris, litter, junk,
Clutter, jumble, mess, sweepings, refuse, ruin, wreckage,
Nonsense spouted, a history of promises as bunk,
Detritus, dross, drivel, claptrap, tripe and garbage,
The trash, the waste, the bull, the bilge, the schlock, the muck
You almost made of us, the riffraff, dregs you drank with,
The filth, the dirt, the scum, slime, shit, crud, crap and fuck,
Ramail, ramayle, ramal, ramel, ramelle,
Rammell, rammal, rammale, rammald, ramaille.
That's all you've left us, all you are to us and all
You'll ever be, not negative or positive,
Nor even nowt, but simply nothing, nothing, nothing.

A Journey by Mandeville

I'm learning the discipline of goodbye.
The last digits on my calculator
Wink backwards like water flowing uphill.
I regard sugar cubes in a wineglass
Beside the coffee percolator which puffs
Evenly like a Frenchman indicating
That something is of no importance.

It is probably the last sound I will hear.
I am signing a contract with a vision
And must whirl away from friendship
In a spiral of wine and boredom,
A red-eyed shift where I stand still and blink
To find myself in another place.

I will enter the republic of light
And relinquish certain customs of speech.
I will live among a people who hear nothing.
A membrane covers their mouths. Their ears
Are no more than faint ridges of skin.

How do they communicate? By touch.
How are they moved? By the scud of clouds
Over giant mirrors set in mountains,
By the quiver of a single hair
Stretched across a hygrometer.
It is a land of careful measurement.
Each man wears a pocket sundial.

How do they love? With heliographs glinting
Across dunes, with waving handkerchiefs.
What do they worship? Not a god but language.
It was something which existed before them.
They remember but cannot prove it.

So will I speak? Yes. But they will consider
My mouth an offence and hurry to seal it.
They will amputate my ears. I will come back
With my eyes glistening like molten lava
In volcanoes. By day I will gesture
In dumbshow, at night signal with torches.

View From a Train

Next to the church where the village gives way to a wood
A statue of the local saint, gloss painted
So his cassock, beard and biretta glow black
Against his white surplice and the scalded pink
Of a hand clasping a rosary whose beads shine like blood.

Beside him is a leafless apple tree
With fruit, each so profoundly steeped in red
The colour leaks into the flesh if they are cut in two.
Above them circle more than a counting rhyme
Of magpies scolding something not at first in view

Before they sweep and glide like paper aeroplanes
Over a field of late, dilapidated maize,
All dust and rustle, to where a group of boys
Have turned their backs on us, pulled down their jeans
And now spank their bottoms, white and pink, at our stalled train.

A Language Shift

Its first name was a derivative of hoot
The first recorded mention was for tax purposes
Describing a place 'by owls beset
Though sheltered from wind and possessing sweet water'.

Medieval obscurity followed until an Igor
Or Bela or Kazimir known as the Belovéd,
Whose last descendant put a pistol to his head
After losing the last vineyard at Monte Carlo,

Built the city known as 'Heart' with its seven hills,
Seven churches, seven fountains, seven bridges
Across the little river and on the walls
Seven towers named after his seven lovely daughters.

Then a Protestant university,
A vernacular bible, military defeat.
Heart was sacked and became a long hurt,
Five of the towers bombarded beyond repair.

The seven bridges still spanned the river
Between the arcades of an absent gentry.
Across the river lived a fearful people
To whom the city burghers forbade entry.

They harmed no one, but the city blamed them for its hurt,
Taxed them double, imagined child sacrifice,
Over a century changed its name to hate
Until supermen arrived and purified the city.

Some acknowledgement of error was conceded,
A power station was constructed, factories:
Heat was the name celebrated by the Party
Until the accident when the river glowed at night.

Slowly the city reverts to its first name 'hoot',
The noises made at the last official party speech,
Wasteland now by owls and rats beset,
The sound at night of trains from X to Y

Heard across the river near the seven bridges
Where the seven lovely daughters of Igors,
Or Belas or Kazimirs sell themselves
For seven million local or seven dollars.

A Roasting Piglet

I gave a lift to a man.
He was slightly the worse for drink
And the mapwork on his face
Showed that he and alcohol were always close.

I gave a lift to a man.
The day was chilly and here
There's little threat from a stranger
Except becoming very drunk.

I drove him to his cabin in the woods.
He invited me for coffee
And pressed a triple vodka on me
Which had to be gulped down in one.

We and his friends watched a piglet
Turning slowly on a metal spit
Driven by a motor with a husky purr
Like a queen cat giving birth.

Elsewhere a government had changed.
Elsewhere NATO prepared to bomb the Serbs.
My man basted and sprinkled herbs
As fat dripped and charcoal sputtered.

The pig's jaws gaped round one end of the spit.
The other end came out through a thigh.
Its legs and trotters were folded back.
It could have knelt for the butcher's knife.

We laughed when my man took a cloth
And wiped bubbles from its fizzing snout.
Its ears crisped, the slash across its throat
Cooked from red to gold. I took my leave.

Elsewhere I had paths to sweep,
Mushrooms to pick beside roaring water.
Elsewhere I had other fish to fry,
A piglet of my own to slaughter.

Cutting Hair in Ruthenia, 1939

Old Hakoš would set out on the veranda wall
A comb, scissors, a china basin, a towel,
A cut-throat razor with a wooden handle,
A mug for coins for those who had a mind
To pay in cash not in kind.

Boys would come, their fathers, their grandfathers,
All of them skinny; harvest yet to be gathered,
Fruit unripe and famine the previous year.
The adults would sit in the yard and smoke,
Drink slivovitz and talk

Of the new regime, a vanished Jew,
Good riddance or *No doctor, what are we to do?*
Or words of regret spoken without undue
Emphasis, informers being everywhere
Then and for many years after,

While the boys went first, the napes of their necks
Clipped to a soft down then shorn bare with a flick
Of a wrist which otherwise placed brick on brick,
Hakoš being the village master builder
Deft with trowel and mortar.

Sixty years on I watch meteors flare
And drop in streaks like blonde and silver hairs.
On the veranda under the moon and stars
I work alone my scissors doing the talking,
Indoors an alarm clock ticking.

Travelling Circus

First of all there's perpetual motion of a sort:
a belly dancer champing gum,
                              waggling her hips
but unable to quiver a single muscle in her torso
on this hot afternoon,
                      a Polish strong man
creaking on his forearms down a set of wooden steps,
a sword swallower straining,
                            tilting back as far as she can
so a small tear becomes a rent then void in her pink tights,
drunken clowns snarling,
                         emptying buckets of paper spite
over the crowd's continual shiftings, shiftings,
cranings of necks,
                   swivellings of heads,
                                         waftings
of the smells of garlic, vodka, children and sweat.

Outside the canvas there's a misery of stillness:
a conglomerate of pythons on a bare bough,
three chimpanzees, grey muzzled, with their teeth knocked out,
a panther inert and scruffy as an old soft toy
dangling its ruined paws over the edge of its jail house
seeing not prairies but the car park behind the city gate
and a truck and trailer with samples from the seven seas,
a ramp and strips of burlap indicating access.

Over the course of sixty feet there's little clarity.
There's cigarette smoke, detergent stink, entropy
and whispers as randomly congregated beings
nudge both sides of tanks of thick green glass.
                                                Anemone,
sand shark, urchin, an octopus overseeing
emptiness from the single stone it has hunched around,
starfish like cut-outs pasted on a classroom window
are not quite odd enough.
                          So in the whispering
that shuffles in and out disappointment can be discerned
– This is the ocean then – .
                             There's no sense of incongruity;

huge vessels of salt water hauled as far as possible
across this continent away from surf and undertow.
I think of the circus moving on,
                              its trucks later found
in a roadside lay-by,
                    all doors open,
                              only a dribble
of stale brine from the tanks and nothing visible
except strange clouds overhead gliding to the sea.

A Word for Lack

They're hardly, if ever, mentioned now,
Those with double eyelids and hair on their palms.
The SS took the village shape-changers away
To a place where they assumed a permanent form.

Fifty years on we hear about a plague of quail
Whose eggs woodsmen injected with cyanide
Which hungry gypsies took from the nest, ate and died
And of a wolf which lapped beer from a pail.

The wolf staggered one night into a hunter's gun.
The quail still crackle from a clump of thorn
With a sound like a dozen newspapers snapped shut
All at once in a room of dust and slanting sunlight.

It'll rain. Fields of maize will lose their powdery look
Becoming green and bronze. The wind won't rustle through
The rows of stalks and drooping leaves but creak
Against tonnages of ripening cobs and moisture.

Grandmamas will gossip about cabbages and kings,
About cottages not kept up with mould upon the linen,
About raspberries to be picked and bottled for the young
Who'll never eat them, about the theft of hens.

Juniper, sloe, apple and ash give way to grass
And then outcrops of rock white as snow which form a peak
Where, as you say, foxes will bid goodnight to us
And the few folk left in a village named from a word for lack.

We trudged up there looking for the uncle of a friend,
An American. Where the road became bare stone
The village's last remaining child cycled up and down
Seemingly indifferent to our demands

To know the number of his house. Then a squawk of gravel
As the bike swerved and braked. The hooded boy or girl
Pointed to an orange garment nailed to an oak
To scare birds off the potato crop. The uncle's coat?

Should we find out now? You fall asleep as it gets dark
Still worrying and leave me in the porch with wine.
Behind me the treadle on the pre-war Singer clacks
As working clothes are made good, seams and buttons sewn.

The hammers click as Jožko cleans his shotgun.
The shepherdess clucks over high school trigonometry.
I drink deeply and gaze at shadow where the river runs,
Where the mill wheel clatters pushed by water's gravity.

An arc of stars begins to rise above the apple trees.
I name their bit of constellation with whatever comes to mind;
The lost uncle, the child's finger, the American friend,
The forgotten stories, the quails' eggs, the wolf's bloodshot eyes.

Observing the Sunrise: From a Letter from Russia

1

I'm on duty today sitting near my father-in-law.
He has cancer, but the operation wasn't radical.

There are only two patients in this ward, the other is between worlds.
He's eaten nothing for days, just drinks, smokes and smells terrible

which is why I'm sitting by the open door to the passage
where I can observe L—'s father. We'll spend the night here.

We must keep an eye on two connections from his body
to a bottle under the bed, a urine collector.

I have a book with me (translated into Russian),
a novel by John Braine called something like *The Way Up The Hill*.

The British mentality is described rather interestingly,
but having no experience I can't say badly or well.

2

I had to stop writing. I had something to do or was far too sleepy.
This is the second night I've been here. So my English forgive and forget.

Some patients with tubes from different parts of their bodies
pass me by from time to time on their way to the toilet.

The nurses changed the dressings on that man between earth and heaven
(or hell). He doesn't smell any more. He's almost arrived wherever.

A nurse on call asked me to wake her when he stops breathing.
It's not very pleasant suddenly to have to watch over

a human being's last moments. Yes, he died a moment ago.
I've just told the nurse, Sister Irina, a pretty girl,

and she's gone to ask another to help carry his body away.
Excuse my naturalism. It's a way to escape this world of Peter Breughel.

3

My father-in-law seems not to have noticed what has happened.
He's one of the most intelligent people in our city.

He was born in Leningrad in 1928.
When the war began he and his sister were evacuated by decree.

But as the result of someone's terrible mistake
they were sent to meet the Germans and their train hit by a bomber.

They escaped safely and got to a village which was not occupied.
He had to work on a kolkhoz and got acquainted with hard labour.

He was going to write a realistic novel about this
and planned to repeat the route they took in 1941.

But he found the documents connected with their adventure
(later evacuations were more successful) had been taken.

4

Having just bought a car I hoped to take him to his weekend home
his *Ebony Tower*, where close to nature he hoped to live and write.

He'd built himself a small house there, 2 by 3 metres.
He'll hardly use it any more or the boat

in which we rowed to the centre of Lake O— and fished
observing the sunrise. Three or four times a year we must have done this.

I will finish this letter with a small tragedy of my own.
The day before I became assistant to a nurse I tried to purchase

a car radio cassette player from a second-hand shop,
but I found it had been robbed and the radio stolen.

Probably it isn't my karma to have a car radio.
My spelling I have checked. My English forgive and forget again.

Grace

Something you won't ever bring pressure to bear on;
wafer on the tongue, sip of wine,
a symbol of nourishment, itself a symbol
of what can't be consumed or felt.
You might wish to say it is like
the way the wind seems to blow light
on cloudy days across the surface of the sea.
You'd be utterly mistaken.

Every Christmas my daughter speaks Old Slavonic
over mushroom and cabbage soup,
over portions of river carp.
I hear, but barely understand.
I barely understand: a true comparison.

After a Quarrel

Three yards of rusty conduit guide
A spring away from a bank of orange shale
So its water curves as a lucid, remorseful cord
Under which I duck my head for the sheer chill.

I am Adam with unoriginal sins,
A plastic bag and a sharp-edged knife.
I pour out a soft hoard for cleaning on to dry flat stones.
There's only the spring's patter and the blurred huff and puff

Of a dog down valley barking at someone harmless
As I sort first through butter mushrooms with brown heads
Oozing a clear fluid smelling of citrus
And then parasols with unopened, flecked, taffeta hoods.

I trim the stalks of what grows overnight
From a tang in the air to love, from love to what must decay.
Beside me a black cricket spreads wings of scarlet,
Flies off making the whirr of a clockwork toy

Towards ravines of beech leaf, pine needle, mud and boulder
Where streams make unseen moral noises of can and should
All the way to the Danube, to the river
Of Good Remembrance or the river of Blood.

On the bank of shale are rampion, forget-me-not,
Harebell, Michaelmas daisies, above me a sky
Luminous as a boy's crystal of copper sulphate:
All are shades of blue for penitence, for apology.

After wrong-headed anger there can be stillness.
What could be the colour or movement of forgiveness?
Up valley a fox crosses with languorous leap and bound
A field of meadowgrass, ash-blonde, combed all ways by the wind.

All Saints' Day

There's colour, too, left wherever we might have come from.
By fences of corrugated iron are red berries of bittersweet,
In backyards late apples, Jonathans by name,
Whose burgundy skin stains through the whole fruit
Whenever we take a kitchen knife and slice them.

There are white chrysanthemum bouquets on the graves
And lilies, glossy as chinaware, in garlands of conifer.
Round them candles in glasses sputter orange flame.
We stand and say nothing. Far from these minutes in our lives
A train makes a sound like a pencil on a piece of paper.

The Blue Company

Some months before the year of revolutions
a late friend took a train into the heartland
of what was held up as a model of despotism;

a stopping train, in his compartment
one other passenger clad in a blue suit
needing thirty minutes' attention from a stiff clothes brush.

Opening a mildly indecent magazine
this other proceeded to masturbate
for two hours of the journey before alighting

at a border post somewhere between pine forest
and pine forest. He was not flagrant, of course,
this was the heart of despotism, but furtive, rubbing

at his groin beneath the magazine.
My late friend tried changing compartments.
The guard checked his place card then scolded him in a language

he could not possibly understand
before ushering him back to his proper place
where the blue suited man sat, his hands folded in his lap.

There was no restaurant car either
where he could have eked out a grainy coffee
and, when he tried standing among the illicit smokers,

cadging a cigarette made of coarse tobacco
and trying not to gag on the acrid smoke
(needless to say my late friend was a non-smoker),

the guard came and relieved him of five Swiss francs
before escorting him back to his proper place
where he remained until the masturbating man alighted.

My late friend spent the time gazing at the trees
trying not to turn his head from pine and pine,
He could not help but hear the crackle of pages, the heavy breathing.

My late friend was a potter who made vases.
Until that journey he had specialised
in a blue glaze the colour of dusk just before the sun sets.

After the journey he never used blue again.
His last works employed a cloud grey, a pitch black,
a translucent white, then no glaze at all, just the colour of raw clay.

There were originally ten of us.
He was the last to keep in touch with me.
Now it is all I can do to keep in touch with myself.

We came together under despotism
in North Africa. The salaries were huge.
We taught, were paid and took our holidays every three months.

We had to wear blue overalls at work:
this due south of Italy beside a bay
where the water was the colour of the Virgin Mary's robes

at least according to one of our company,
the third to depart from common knowledge
in the back of a police van waving and shouting, 'I love you all!'

We got our overalls the day after we arrived
and somehow let ourselves be called the Blue Company.
I forget whose idea it was. We held together for three weeks;

about the length of any decent revolution.
Longer and it becomes either a bore or terror.
Remember your first taste of ice cream then think of it

being served as dessert ever after
or an unattainable love telephones
to say, 'I want you', then calls again and again and again.

The first of us to go had to be sedated
three weeks into our twelve-month contract.
Every night he screwed up pieces of blue toilet paper

and dropped them outside his bedroom door.
'So I can hear the CIA,' he said,
'when they come to silence me before I tell exactly what I know.'

The second resigned through extreme boredom.
I've already told you about the third
and the fourth did a runner on his first leave with his girlfriend.

The fifth had agreed to do only six months.
The sixth did not return from a second leave
and was found murdered, floating in an Amsterdam canal.

The seventh left after a year with enough
to furnish his pottery studio.
The eighth, the eighth? I can't even remember what he looked like.

The ninth and I, the tenth, finished a second year.
We last saw each other in Vienna
in a brothel, each with the girl we'd chosen for the night.

I had to pay for his beer and pretzels.
As I've indicated, the potter kept in touch.
I think of the Blue Company as history's exemplar

not only for our three weeks of coincidence
but for our louche provenance, our failure
to be any sort of unity; history as simple craziness,

regretted boredoms, desertions, murder,
continual lapses from credence,
forgotten deeds, forgotten actors, decline and fall.

I'm tempted to confess that I was an agent,
that it's quite incredible the money
you can make for information on harmless remittance men.

But I never was that vile a bastard.
I just recall ten men dressed in blue overalls
under a blue sky by the blue sea. Five of us had blue eyes.

I have the last blue vase made by my late friend.
I think of the year of revolutions as a vase
sky-blue among my textures of parquet and leather upholstery.

I think of clouds passing across the vase's
glazed surface and slipping out of sight
round its plump corners to reappear, never ever the same

shape of cloud, never the same shop
for that blouse my wife wanted, never ever
the same ship sailing over the porcelain curve of the horizon

At Huwailah Beach

By the village, *Mother of the Pillars*,
We gave a lift to an Egyptian peasant
Whose speech was corrupt with Hindu phrases.
He tickled the back of my neck with a snake

Which he'd hidden in voluminous sleeves.
Not venomous, it sidewound down my shirt.
Its head was small as a fingerjoint
And it coiled on my knees neat as a cat.

The road was dark so we invited him to stay.
Now he rocks from side to side as someone
Picks out *Brown Girl in the Ring* on the oudh
Tapping the striped belly of the instrument.

Fins flicker in the shallows as fish twist
Tugged in by handlines. Soon they will be grilled
And eaten over a quarrel about
Where the best Arabic is spoken

While I go through a box of Kleenex
Since I have the Gulf War all over my feet.

In the Harbour at Leptis Magna

An octopus unfolds like a dishcloth
Then mottles to the colour of the sand
And seagrass it undulates upon.
Its clear childish eyes which regard me
As a kind of Zeppelin with flippers
Make it a gentle owl of water
More bird than Minerva's chipped emblem
Which heat and wind have left hardly winged,
Hardly clawed, an idiocy of stone
Perched on a plinth among thorns and arches.

Dumb as a dead language it presides
Where the breeze is a ruin of the voice
Shifting dunes over the buried two-thirds
Of this Roman monument to force,
Rustling, carrying nothing to hint
How gossip, sonorous with profit
From olive oil, in those avenues
I wandered through an hour ago, dwindled
To the whimper of a few scared townsfolk
Sending their sons out on the last ship.

I was not detained. It was too hot
And an Arab followed to make sure
I left with nothing which was not mine.
He looked away as I stripped to trunks
And waded backwards into the harbour
Where now I float above the gaze
Of what survives. Around me little fish
File as their ancestors must have done
After galleys which were wrecked, scuttled
Or simply rowed out of sight long ago.

The Drowned Boy

i.m. Munji Mohammed Abu Derbalah

Yesterday wind snarled through the square
As his friends brought chairs and hung out lamps
For mourning in the lee of his flat.
We sat informally in silence
As lights jerked in the gale seeming
To founder in the sand. I bore it
For half an hour while some sat all evening
Preferring respect to comfort.

Today what we are left with is ground
Damped down, pitted with the marks of chairs.
Where the square is dry, pythons of sand
Slide as the wind eddies to stillness.
We taste grit and wait for the sky to clear.
The boy is with habits of saying
Yesterday. He recedes into the words
Of inadequate regret, but remains

An acrid ripeness in our language,
A woodsmoke curling through the village,
A memory whose truth alters
Like perspective among a grove of palms
Where the air is hazy with dust
So the trees seem to form the relic
Of a temple, their branches arching
Broken apses on marble pillars.

How much of him can we take with us?
As much as we take of ourselves.
The future narrows to a catwalk
Over the dangerous places
And reaches boats whose sails are sewn
From winding sheets. They bob on a sea
Calm as brass although now we hear it
Unappeasable, nuzzling the rocks.

Delays

Some of the redeemed are queuing
For the last test of their patience.
They wait behind double glazing
While an officer telephones
For air tickets and exit visas.

The rest of us have two months to wait;
Months of light, olives, soft drinks,
The listlessness induced by heat
While clouds coalesce out of the day's
Perpetual misunderstanding.

They accumulate and hover
As if wanting to be bargained down.
Beneath them birds cluster on wire
Twittering, a sound which collects
All our ways of saying *Yes* or *No*

And migrates taking our chances
Of being answered as the clouds
Vanish leaving no more
Than wet ground, a stain on the day's
Routine of things failing to occur.

We begin with sentences of hope.
We require certain household items,
Cement for the crevice through which
Ants pour, a washer for a tap.
But the most we can achieve

Is an idiom for killing time.
Our grammar is slowly bleached
Of a past and future which become
A secret diction to interpret
What we are supposed to think.

Somewhere is an archive where requests
Ripen, are harvested and lost
While delays gather until they change
Into what we ask for but now find
Impossible to accept.

How should we describe delays;
As a jam of vehicles
Leaving Tripoli, blaring home;
As an avalanche of stone
Shifted by water greasing rock?

No. They mass like inclement weather
In the evening. But we are sleeping
When they break and shed everything
We need. Dreaming, we can hear
Only the rattle of jalousies,

Imagine only the tankers
Dipping at anchor, the rockets
Swaying on their bases. By morning
The responses to our pleading
Glisten on barley in the fields

Or remain as dampness in the sand
Underneath our feet. By noon
They have faded as we walk by,
Parched of speech, of expectation,
While chickens chatter in Arabic.

Sonnets from Zawia

On Cooking Chickens

1

The newcomers and their families wait
For the Zawia bus. It's their first chance
To do a little more than appreciate
This place of wind and abundance
Where spray from irrigation water swirls
And grit is driven hard enough to bruise
The scrubbed faces of British wives, still girls
So young they talk excitedly of shoes.

How long before their husbands worry
That many of us are single men
As we mention shortages and hurry
To advise on where to school a daughter
And how to hasten the plucking of a hen
By putting it in boiling water?

2

Some hens struggle under a seat.
Their wings thud against the leather
Rhythmically like a hanged man's feet.
Minutes ago they crowded together
Tied with a green flex which hobbled
Their legs so only their heads could blink
From side to side as they gobbled
Imagined grain. Too tired to think
We carry to the coach the best
Cuts of meat, loaves and potatoes.
Our driver rises from his rest
Next to a well in which he throws
His cigarette while sunlight clings
To stone blurring the form of things.

3

Now the light relinquishes its grip
On architecture and the glazed, lopped heads
Of bullocks piled along the butcher's strip
Where we bargained for glossy sweetbreads.
Our driver has a gentle villainy
Jolting us home through date palms which ripen
To a sticky brown. We think of money
Or argue how to cook a Libyan hen.
Could we be called down to earth? We are less
Than the dusk is with its lack of light,
Reduced more than we'd care to confess
To these newcomers waving us goodnight
As we wither away from them while they stand
Dangling a live bird in each free hand.

Evening

In front of me hawks squeal and must swoop
Around the water tower. They aren't clear forms
But lines of flight inscribed above a loop
Of sea tinted by the first winter storms
Which quiver soundlessly miles away.
Close to me the tamarisk branches seem
Flaws in the dusk's raw silk or else they sway
From an ageing Japanese artist's dream
Of touch made visible. But nightfall
Takes that royal luminous idea
Leaving me only able to recall
From the minute republic of the ear
As tomcats squabble on the garden wall
And cockroaches whistle in the hall.

The Mediterranean

The body politic shakes within a change
Of mood. What he was promised now becomes
A might-have-been. But he preferred the strange
And left home. The strange was strange. So he thumbs
His way back to original design.
His mother's words come to flood him with excess
Like hormones accelerating a decline.
Will he be reborn and achieve success?
Perhaps. The sea is ageing and impure.
In media terra her glad blue eye
Wrinkles in its orbit to ensure
His handsome middle age where he can lie
Upon a beach between her infected calms
And a fly-blown future under palms.

The Fifth Man

Clouds must have built up since no glints show
As I stroll outside after listening
To a relative on the radio
Confess his treachery of years ago.
At the newcomers' flat a chicken screams
Strangled behind jalousies glistening
With drizzle. It's a night when dreams
Will turn hints dropped in childhood to themes
For fairy tales where a wicked uncle
Makes a lost father seem magical
Though the broadcast should not mean much to me,
Noticed rather as if an animal
Had whimpered above the whisper of the sea
Which is unconcerned, random, free.

Literacy

The calligraphy of cloud above me
Embroiders the Arabic word for rain
While a hoopoe casts an economy
Of shadow swaying, like a weathervane,
On power lines. My worst pupil passes
With a hawk upon his wrist. He makes me look
At the bird and his new pair of glasses.
For eighteen months he has read 'black' as 'book'.
'Now reading good,' he claims and indicates
His cataract and the hawk's uncovered
Chilling eyes. He stoops to sniff a pinion
As water's alphabet evaporates
Over that valley where he discovered
More than thirty species of scorpion.

Month of Fasting

A scorpion crawls beneath my mattress.
Its tail flickers like a gas jet
When I brush it into a plastic bin.
It gives me something to gossip about
As clouds lower and earth and sea compress
Ramadan to hours in which I sweat
Unused, yet paid for all of it. I grin
Like a monetarist 'toughing it out'
Since I know the sea breeze will lift the press
Of slick air, upturn my mosquito net,
Creak shutters against their hooks and begin
To challenge a hush so complete I'd doubt
Anything moved if it weren't for the sound
Of the scorpion scuttling round and round.

Spring in the Desert

Like awkward deer, tentatively greedy
For sugar, girls sidle close then run
Giggling to their mothers while we make fun
Of our friend, the policeman Al Hamidi,
Gesturing to a mountain shattered by heat,
Swept bare by flashflood, a ruined face
Staring at this green, Gaddafi's perfect place
Where no family picnic is complete
Without a father crouching to cut stocks
Of fodder for his sheep as stereos play,
Shining like tiny silver tower blocks,
And where each group, as far as the eye can see,
Has a son or daughter who stands up to sway
To a song from Radio Tripoli:
      'By the rivers of Babylon
      There we sat down,
      Yea, we wept,
      When we remembered Zion.'

In Libya

I have just sponged the walls and floors clean
Of the blood of a retiring teacher
Who has left to study Applied Linguistics.
He was alone in the village. Four students
Demanded sex and broke a glass in his face
When he refused. Some say he had it coming.
The students have been sent to the army.

His blood does not whimper for revenge.
It was rank. Ants trekked between clots and their nest.
Yards away the Mediterranean
Seems blue as iodine and flat as lint
Although others have made it a prairie
Where a cattle baron rides against
A mean bible-punching herder of sheep.

There might be a hero, who loves a schoolmarm
And is kind to bargirls, bringing an end
To their range war. But he'd be shot in the back
Before he could pull a gun and, besides,
Such justice is a dream of the helpless
Whose trust is a vice. The only virtue
Is to be candid about one's compromise.

My tapes give a choice of music from Dowland
To the Flying Lizards. Something from between them
Will echo in the garden when I sprinkle
Water on the teacher's tomatoes, sweet pea,
Mint, cantaloupe, sunflowers and nightstock.
Will I do this from pity or guilt?
From neither. I like plants and hate waste.

You may photograph me stooped over
The plot of sand and fertiliser
And make myths of simplicity
As imagined by Augustus in Virgil
Or retired politicians in themselves.
But please note my irritated smile,
My youthful figure, my lack of fear.

The Country of Rumour

The country of rumour is fertile.
Sprinklers shake like wands from irrigation pipes
Whirling magic circles over alfalfa,
Among orange groves and rows of olive
Far from the stretches of brittle sand.
It is a country held by a love or hope
Who never makes herself clear, who rises
Like the sun freckled with lilac cloud.

Later drizzle streaks our faces then lifts,
A rustle diminishing like sentences
Murmured, misunderstood, having only said
'Perhaps. Tomorrow. Why not?' while we look up
As if we'd heard 'I've been waiting so long
For you to speak.' But we are dazzled
By silent light pouring down on power lines,
Cool villages, their ridges of husbandry,
Their horses hobbled to a grazing patch.

Few messages arrive and if they do
Are handed to us in the dark with nudges.
All the letters have the date 'If it were
The twentieth of June' and from them falls
A scent of meaning in a writing yellow
As mimosa. Our envelopes contain
Lint which wrapped a confiscated gift.

More news is got from ruins near the sea
Where the amphitheatre accepts signals
From the stars like a radio telescope.
On its columns the conqueror's script
Has all but been erased by visitors,
By lovers who scrawl forbidden likenesses
Of friends in charcoal, by the devotee
Muttering 'Allah, Allah' in the forum.

Here statues of lions are pocked with salt
And could be slinking back to their first form
Or becoming clearer, a honed savagery.
Here there is no shape for the future
And the past is used circumspectly
For a killing or an accident.

Galleys from Rome have come and disembarked
To sow the ground of Carthage with bitterness.
Submarines will dive for the last time
Leaving a radioactive sadness.
But the word of God is ever present.
It sobs from minarets five times a day
Inland from a sea which feeds quietly,
A lean blue lion munching upon stone.

Maps have never been drawn for the country
Of rumour. Compass needles refuse
To point. They curl like worms beneath the glass.
Only the scarab beetle's path traces
A track in dust wider than a finger,
Only a butterfly fans wings patterned
Like a river delta, only ants arched
Like ballet dancers have horizons
Definitive as a mountain range.

In the country of rumour we lose our names.
In our passports photographs discolour
To sepia showing the forehead,
Whiskers and frockcoats of ancestors.
Our identity cards have signatures
Which run to liquid and read backwards.
Our hands have palms whose lines are smoothed away.
We show them to policemen as proof
Of innocence and to each other
Whispering 'Are you French? Are you English?
Are you Czech? Are you Italian? Are you –?'

Sunrise at the Wadi Nisah

On the mesa opposite
A single bird of prey
Dusts each outcrop with its shadow.
It slowly searches high above
A conclave of carrion crows
Who deliberate uneasily

As I clamber up a ridge
Leaving canny adulterers
From the north of England who lie
Beyond unemployment and their wives
In the arms of Irish nurses.
If the Saudi police should come …

Someone, sleepless and uncoupled
Plays a cassette of the Boomtown Rats.
It blares over scattered vehicles
While I gaze into a valley
Music and transport cannot reach
So steep are the sides, so definite

The water courses scoring its floor.
It is like a cracked cup which leaks
Or an enormous palm of a hand
With lines of destiny,
Incisions of the head and heart
Complicated beyond belief.

It is not a place for those
Needing the sound of water
Though the consequence of rain is here
Slashing the gradual processes
Of wind and heat so that even stones
Seem to rest between rage and torpor.

But it is a place where Arab poets
Used to meditate on love.
The great wadi twists delicately
Between dunes whose little roundness
Is luscious as the shoulders
Of a girl on her wedding night.

Over them the sunlight oozes
Like an oil made from apricots
While a breeze, lacking scent or moisture,
Flows across the landscape
Cooling me so I look away
From the stink and sweat of my own kind.

An Execution in Riyadh

He kneels, head hunched between his shoulders,
His muscles superstitious contracting him
In this involuntary crouch. His body,
Not his mind, tries a useless magic.
There is no way he can avoid the death
From the dagger and the sword whose sheen
Is rival to the more permanent sun
And to which European women in the crowd
Bow their heads as they focus their cameras.
A cut: he does not move. His body is stubborn.

Students take benzedrine the night before
An examination they will fail.
Men transplant single follicles of hair
Over months. The rhino is killed off
For its horn powdered to preserve the youth
Of rich Cantonese. And sillier millionaires
Are deep frozen in old age until such time
Death is cured. Visceral or thought out
An impulse to live huddles in them all
Shielding its neck. A second cut: he does not move.

Once a man crouched for two hours stiff with fright.
The crowd grew bored or fainted in the heat.
Then toppling forward his body straightened
From its posture of shame into acceptance.
A third cut and his head jerks back. The blade sinks,
A steely coolness severing the stifling air
Returning to the executioner's side,
Point resting in the dust, hardly stained.
The women shudder and take picture
After picture of the spout of blood.

English for Special Purposes

Looking through the videotapes:
Hand Grenades: Some Do's and Don'ts,
Biological Operations,
I recall an argument
Between students on the Taif road.
Our car had broken down
Near a solar telephone.

Its blue panels tilted to the sun
And it had an aerial
For signals on microwave.
It seemed to unify
Sunlight with technology.
We admired its elegance
As we waited for help to come.

Then Fahad smirked and pointed
Ibrahim is a black man.
His grandfather was slave to mine,
To which he added quickly,
Kul an-nas abd'ullah.
It was odd how such a piety
Could bring instant silence

Though Ibrahim had the last word
Whispering that Fahad's head was shaved
By the religious police
Who caught him following girls
Round Execution Square
Whose pavements were thick with clippings
As the open space was hosed clean.

I think of the open wounds and burns
I'll show them in the film on Safety
Which I'll use to illustrate
A lesson with *must* and *should*
ENGLISH FOR SPECIAL PURPOSES
You must be careful with
Electricity and sharp instruments.

How do I teach? Certainly not,
Despite my teaching aids,
So we might all acquire
The same habits of indifference.
Yet I've sold myself or else
Was bought, perhaps unknowingly.
I'm an instrument with charm,

A bland educator with nothing
In my brief on good and evil.
And what do I teach? Certainly not
That our separate grammars hide
Similar minds which bear the birthmarks
Violence and Domination,
Gods we might all be slaves of.

Mimicking unities
Of nature and artifice
I transmit useful forms.
Looking through the videotapes
I devise catchier titles,
Shrapnel can make you wise,
Chemicals and germs make you free.

Note: *Kul an-nas abd'ullah* can mean 'Everyone is a slave of God'.

Clouds

Bored or fascinated all turn a face,
An unlikeness, to clouds and interpret
The almost-castle, the almost-clown's head.
What is it they show just to you and me?
Each billow repeats the wheel of moisture,
Heat and air over the sea, over earth.
Yet for us clouds salute the mirror
Which the flecked world is, flow on, part of us,
Intangible as our meanings become
When words that we let fall away irritate,
Drive listeners indoors or are taken
For granted even when clouds are exact
Furrowing the blue like ridges of sand,
Massing like wood anemones, scarring
The horizons that have been torn apart ...

Then we command, *Recognise! Recognise!*
The indifferent heads hardly look up
Or else mildly observe, *You could be right.*
We need a generation that will walk
Bareheaded through the rain. Just now I hear
Guns or thunder, no way of telling which,
As air quivers like liquid in a glass
Beneath this blank possession of the sky.
There is no flash heavenwards or earthbound.
The light lies muted like a scolded child.
A little way away a radio
Is choked off and my companions
Cease their grumbling about lunch and taxis.
(One is bankrupt and must work abroad for a wife
Who is unfaithful. The other saves to trawl for boys.)

Awkward friend, you, too, must settle among
The failing and the different and wait
For certain weathers to vanish or break.
Just now, as I wait, soldiers are crouching
Beyond me in African marigolds.
They hold fruit and Kalashnikov rifles.
Beyond them are the portioned distances
Of smallholdings, accumulations blurring
To colours which might be tamarisk, olive, maize.
And, so far from me in expectation,
So far from me in your lack of terror,
In the direction of where you can choose
Other elements for a temperature
All must feel or die, clouds begin to close
Gaps above the blue crayon of the sea.

Translation

After midnight, after midnight
The owls home in. They are late lovers
In this damp year so clamour
Tenderly when we approach
Their nesting place. Once I was calm.

After midnight, after midnight
The owls drift over meadows
Their whimpering cut short when they drop
Like doodlebugs on mice, on kittens
On the common speech of hedgerows.

Once I said I wanted nothing.
But after midnight, after midnight
I am translated to a stammer
Of desire, finding a voice I'd thought
No more than stern is now gentle.

After midnight histories are changed.
Old wars are whispers and our arms
Holding each other in astonishment.
The owls challenge us from a lime tree.
We say the password mouth to mouth.

You leave your touch aching in my shoulders,
Your scent fading slowly in a shirt.
My thoughts are in the soft words of owls.
A German accent like a lullaby
Wakes me after midnight, after midnight.

Travels in Desire

It should have been called Famish,
Full of eye-tricks and appetites;
Palace walls finished with render
Pocked and gaudy as egg custard,
The emperor's crown a nougat
Of gold and the Holy Spear
A candy stick. On such deceits
You break eye-teeth and your heart.

They called it their musical city.
Someone in the room next to mine
Cleared his throat before spitting,
The sound a double-bass might make
Being tuned up for a waltz.
A girl tinkled on the phone
In a gentle Austrian accent
Like a harpsichord, *How black are you?*

Under my breath I muttered
Them bones, them bones, them dry bones,
And rattled my lucky pebbles
All to no avail. I received
Formal answers when I needed work.
It shows in the art they've kept;
Saint Sebastian painted as stone
Which bleeds, bound against blonde marble,

Shot through with arrows criss-crossing
To make a trellis of pain.
The archers have muscly buttocks
And vanish over a hill
To a town of clay and wattle
Where, no doubt, they *take one beer*
And a quick screw against a fence
Which collapses with mud and squeals.

I vanished over a continent
To a city of wood and water
Whose only stone floats on mist,
Domes like bosoms dressed in silk.
I saw a hair of the Prophet
In a case of brass. Then, stepping out
Into sunlight bristling like a beard
Dyed orange after pilgrimage,

I met a girl from the island, Plenty,
Whose skin was glossy as caramel.
Her promises weren't sweetmeats
But softness, grass after rain.
I gave her my lucky pebbles
And she crossed her feet behind my back.
Call me the Virgin Mary, she said
Gripping with thighs as hard as stone.

Heliopolis

Heaps of rubbish, trellises for summer grapes,
Pomegranate flowers shiny as lipstick,
The usual enlightened self-interest
Of cats seated equally from one another,
The turquoise flash of a tram's connecting rods,
A girl so stone-like in her thought she fails
To wipe away a mascara of small flies
And from the telephone your infuriating
Languorous denial –
                    Maybe I cannot
Come to you today;
                    I wait and wait.
Yesterday I uncovered you and lifted hair
In whose blackness shone lights of mauve and blue
To touch the soft ivory of breasts and shoulders
While someone rang the doorbell over and over.

Afterwards you washed yourself so your brothers
Would not detect any taint of me, made-up,
(Your lips were red as pomegranate flowers –
You must not kiss me now!)
                    disappeared
As the colours shrivelled and the sunset
Call to prayer ground out its syllables.
You left me to the night oxygen of plants,
The territorial disputes of cats,
The groan of iron wheels on sunken rails
And from the rooms beneath me the weeping
Of someone with hurts no one came to cure.

A Little Rain in Riyadh

A drizzle tickles our upturned faces,
Its touch as yet undistressing,
No great disorder but a first
Mild challenge to what we thought we knew.

Would that this settling ghost of water,
Brushing our skin, could provoke something more
Than speculation about volcanoes
Or the fixing of drops round dust.

But as the rain dissolves above the ground
Feeling dwindles like moisture in the air.
Here even our tears dry before we weep.
Our eyes trickle a salt of knowingness.

The skyline shivers like a silent film
Projected on a smudgy cotton screen.
Its flickering accentuates lamplight,
The square façades and angular shadow

Cast in those spaces which lie between us.
Possibility becomes unpeopled.
It is a geometry made by chance
In this city without addresses

Where the young dial randomly
To chatter to anyone about love,
Where a stranger waits like a salesman
In a German car outside your door.

His prospectus shows what you might be
Running from. Beautiful, sweet friend
Do not ever listen to him.
His phrases are a parched nonsense,

A pestle clicking in a mortar
With poisoned grain, coins of iron
Clinking from hand to hand, the rockers
Of empty cradles clacking on stone floors.

We need substantial waters to sense
Anything more than unlikelihoods;
For you the immense, quiet animal
Of the Nile whose night glimmering

Terrifies as you walk beside it;
For me the ocean in the early morning
Relaxed as a sleeper who dreams well.
I think of impossibilities;

Of you opening an umbrella
Against English weather; of you
Regarding me as you would the light shed
Over the sea at Alexandria.

Drought

I've opened the *National Geographic*
At an article on Eritrea
With photographs whose caption reads
Amna Mohammed and her two grandsons
Travelled three days by camel in search of food.
Along the way the boys' mother died.
The photographer has made them elegant:
Limbs like parts of varnished furniture
Arranged half in, half out of shade.
The grandmother's red dress and headscarf
Bloom against the woven wall of the lean-to.
The little boy is covered by a white cloth,
But the older one is naked and sleek flies
Like brown sultanas mass around his anus.
Behind his head are empty, zinc dishes
Scoured absolutely clean so they shine.

Fresh from the shower you compose yourself
Exactly, a gleaming, water-pampered flesh
Whose curve has been perfected by desire.
As you stretch back and look at me I notice
Edges of a petal of a rose after rain.
Are you hungry? you whisper. Then, seeing me
Hesitate, you cover yourself
Until I move fearful of further questions:
Do you still want me?
What have you been reading?

Belly Dancer Weeping

After Picasso – Woman Weeping

I but melted sugar on my legs like a bride,
Not for marriage, but for dancink in ze club.
Ze sweetness dries and I beel it off
So ze hairs lie wiz crystals on ze towel.

Once I butted sugar on all over,
Even on my face which glittered in ze mirror
Until I standed, frowned and flicked my hibs
So somesink shivered from me like soft glass.

It was for a weekend wiz my boyfren.
I said, *Look, Darlink, my skin is smooz*
For ze weddink night! He said, *You're too bale*
Like unbaked bread. Why don't you sunbaze?

I'd went black! Zough for him my colour didn't count.
He liked me for my lonk black hairs and eyes.
He bromised to return from London and buy a house.
Zat was years ago. Now I need ze moneys.

My flesh is blumber, but good enough to eat.
I dress my flesh in stribs of turkoys, bink
And tanksherine. My hairs tankle to my waist.
My breasts and belly ribble for applause.

Tonight, quickly as a disco dancer,
A millionaire will jig-jig on me;
Zat's ze way I like it! Uh-huh! Uh-huh!
Zough I will sink a sonk my boyfren teached me;

My smiles will go. I was kissink him
So didn't heard eggsakly, but I sink it was
Smiles to go zough bromises I keeb
And zen I sleeb, or maybe, *Zen I weeb.*

South District, Prague

One day perfect love could come to me
Like a woman from a crowded bus
Long overdue and driven carelessly
Along an asphalt road wet with rain.

She might travel past untended fields
Which wind has combed so grass lies flat.
I will change the dull, official name
On maps to read *The District of the Heart*.

Today you gesture at sunlight sinking
In the windows of the building opposite.
The sky itself seems blank, uncoloured,
The texture of undyed linen mat.

We watched the glory in the glass spread out
Making concrete seem delicate as coral.
You murmured your favourite English word,
Impossible, impossible,

And refuse my offer of a rose.
How could I explain it to my man?
I wave goodbye at a brilliant smile
On the last bus westwards to a steel town.

One day perfect love could come to me
Like wind blowing snow across the grass.
A shadow with a brilliant smile
Will descend from an empty bus.

Impossible, she'll say as I hold out
Her favourite pink rose and a petal drops,
Then another in the frost. *Impossible*,
She'll breathe, her lips withering my lips.

The Melon Girl

Salim has a harelip and cleft palate.
His father was not advised or was too harsh
To have the defect stitched just after birth.

At school he was not allowed to read
The Holy Qu'ran and his father beat him
His speech being an offence to God.

The other trainees torment him, too much,
For he hurled a chunk of red hot steel
Across the welding shop and so was banned.

Now I have him for one-to-one English.
He lisps *I can only thay Bithmillah,*
Behind a spray of garlic and couscous

Then speculates about my sisters.
Are they virgin? No woman would have him.
He is disgusting and I am ashamed.

For after one too many references
To sisters I said *In the name of God,*
Why don't you try a melon! and he flinched

As though my words had struck him like flung metal.
For thirty days he responded only
To my formal grammar exercises.

Then he told me. *Mister, I tried the melon,*
Dreaming of the perfect girl, bint arba'tash,
The full moon. She had white skin and black eyes.

When I finished my bed was wet with blood
Not melon juice and all through the night
I saw her crying. I became afraid

And hid the broken melon in the earth.
Now every night she stands beside my bed
Thin with crying and I cannot sleep.

Ladies of the Bundesrepublik

Gisela is drinking sekt with Anna,
The expert in holiday romances,
And Gabby who spends a weekend every month
With a Parisian engineer.

Gisela is much younger and so
Calls herself *only a student of love*.
She wants to talk or be advised
Or brag about her Englishman.

Anna and Gabby find him cosy
And tender adds Gisela thinking
How he has underwear of good quality
Something she didn't expect in Englishmen.

They sit almost under two beach umbrellas
Beside the pool. Shade covers their mouths
And gloves them to the elbows so they are like
Nurses in an isolation ward.

The sunlight is also of good quality.
But Gisela is thinking of last winter
When they walked along avenues where steam
Plumed from the drains like pampas grass.

There she complained of her marriage saying
The gravedigger had married a midwife.
The Englishman sighed *Oh Gisela*.
Anna and Gabby are shaking their heads

As she leaves them to bounce on the springboard
Before she dives. Water clasps her.
She giggles when thoughts of her Englishman
Tickle the soles of her feet with their tongues

Babbling *Oh Gisela*. As she rises
Gabby is writing to her Frenchman.
Anna is remembering an Arab
She met in Djerba. She guzzles her drink.

Rainoo Repeats Her English in Bombay

Rainoo dresses and combs her hair.
On the wall there is a scrap of broken glass
Which she uses as a mirror.
If she stands up straight she can see
Her eyes and lips when she puts on rouge and kohl.
If she bends her knees she can see
Her eyes again and her thick, black hair
Which she piles and pins on top of her head.
This is something she does every day.

Rainoo murmurs the English she picked up
In a house in the Persian Gulf.
A yellow-haired Englishwoman taught
The children who listened, sometimes.
Rainoo listened all the time
As she carefully cleaned the schoolroom.
Do you understand, children? Please listen!
Rainoo is listening, aren't you?
Rainoo is good at languages.
This was something the teacher said every day.

There were flowers in the schoolroom.
They used to close when Rainoo touched them.
The master of the house used to touch her.
What didn't he used to touch?
Rainoo used to close like a flower.
She used to close her mouth and turn her head
When he pulled her sari to her waist.
This was something he used to do every day.

Rainoo tucks a rupee inside her bra
For the bus she takes to the brothel.
She walks with a limp from the time
The mistress of the house surprised her
With the master and pushed her downstairs.
This was something she did only once.
Rainoo's passport was stamped with a word for *whore*.
Today Rainoo will speak Marat'hi,
Hindi, English, Arabic and French.
What language won't she speak today?
This is something she does every day.

Pariah

Close to me the other Englishmen
Flirt with each other's wives and ask
Uneasily if I mind their smoking.
I feel they wish I were not here.
A father scolds a son who offers me
A glass of lemonade. *I'm sorry*,
Says the boy, *I'm sorry that you're sick.*

This morning my class debated
If it were entirely right for me
To swim in the month of Ramadan.
Water might pass between my lips,
Water which unbelievers pissed in.
I said I did not think that swimming pools
Were mentioned in the Holy Book.

Six hours to go before my first sip
And I waste myself with looking
At a Spanish girl whose figure's gone.
She holds her child away and speaks to him.
Her stolid body wavers under water
Not heavy any more for a face
Which is wide-eyed. She is beauty now.

Six hours and I will drink just water
Intent upon the Sura for Paradise.
Then I'll wander to that part of town
Whose name translates as *Star* and for the night
I'll hire my Indian girl again.
Her breasts seep milk for her dead son.
Her upper lip sports a slight moustache.

Customer

I could not comfort her. She fell asleep
In tears for her dead son. She awoke
In tears when I put money by the lamp
And kissed the lilac flesh where she gave birth.

There must have been a peep-hole. Her pimp came in
When she tried to give the money back.
He waved an ornamental dagger.
You can't return. She likes you far too much.

I should be fifty years ago
With felt hat and walking stick to hide
My ill-at-ease. I stroll bare-headed
By the bread shops and think of Eros Island

Where water winds its tongue around my waist
And in the hollow under every rock
Are tiny girls, black-eyed, clean as lizards.
Unblinking, they lie absolutely still.

The Spirit is Moved in Old Amsterdam

Have I descended to the wrong place?
My name is Gloria, says the girl
Dressed in a leather corset studded with metal,
Black-haired, black-eyed with a sullen face.

All kinds of whips and canes are tied in sheaves.
On the bed is a piece of cord frayed at the ends
Long enough or short enough to secure my hands.
Surgical gloves dangle from a hook like bleached leaves.

In the middle of the room tied to a post
Are a Yorkie, a Peke and a Bouvier pup.
140 pounds when he grows up.
I call them Father, Son and Holy Ghost.

I am the whole of existence, a midwife
Who gives the slap which expels the first breath
Or the tender nurse who's in at the death
For your last gasp, the easing away of life.

What you might want is not a crime.
Pain is another word for pleasure.
Fifty guilders down at your leisure,
Fifty more and I will take my time.

The Bedu Soldier's Tale

I was absent without leave
On the run from the National Guard.
I had a job in the farmer's souk
Where the bargaining was hard.

Her servant bought Al Ahsa dates
And dropped her number on the ground.
I put my foot on the paper
After carefully looking round.

Six weeks we chatted on the phone
Until her husband went abroad.
She sent her driver in the Rolls
One night when she was bored.

She opened the steel gates herself,
But paused at the hinges' creak.
Moonlight, the breeze, her soft hand's touch
Were wine to one who is weak.

She took me to her daughters' room
In case her brothers came to call.
Three little girls lay like dolls
Covered by an English shawl.

She took me to her daughters' room.
Her husband was abroad to get
A second wife to give him sons.
Otherwise we'd not have met.

On a rug beside the bed she raised
Her plump, white Syrian feet
And, so her voice would not be heard,
Held her veil between her teeth.

Four times I had her quietly
And was about to try again
When a daughter whimpered, *Momma!*
Suffering or dreaming pain.

Quickly she led me back outside.
The Rolls crept up like a hound.
The Tamil driver took me home,
Drove off without a sound.

Since then she has not phoned.
Perhaps she carries my son.
She'll sulk over the second wife
Saying, *Look! God's will is done!*

Soon I'll marry into my tribe,
Grow sleek from good food and forget
Her eyes and the veil between her teeth,
But not, God forgive me, yet.

There Once Was A King of Hungary

From a Slovak folk song

There once was a king of Hungary
of maidens a real deceiver

Every daughter he had laid low
but the mayor's daughter did not wish to know

From a granny weeding her garden
he coaxed advice and begged her pardon

Dress yourself in a maiden's gown
with gloves as white as a goose's down

Go and on the door give a rap
The mayor himself will open up

And when it was after dinner
The mayor spoke unto his daughter

Go, Anička, make up the bed
With this lady you'll lay your head

I've never heard though I've thought deep
that ladies should with maidens sleep

And when the stroke of midnight fell
Anička starts for help to yell

And over the passing of a week
Every day did Anička weep

Then a month and a few days more
Anička wept till her eyes were sore

And after a year had passed by
Anička sang a lullaby

Hushaby baby my little lad
A king of Hungary is your dad

Three Girls and Three Widowers

The man leaning on the railing of the balcony opposite,
Cigarette in hand, is waiting for his wife to die,
The third death in as many months.

The first widower was left with a Pekinese called Martina
And a caravan round and white as a snooker ball.
He takes it to the lake on fishing trips.

The second has an even smaller dog that he's trained to growl
Like a Dobermann in an evil, property-protecting mood.
He drinks rum and neglects a garden

Filled with raspberry canes and red and black currant bushes.
His walnut tree curves over our road, a green awning hung with nuts
Whose rinds stain one's fingers a nicotine yellow.

I practise the phrase you've taught me to express condolences
Though the latest gossip is not about death but about three girls
In a flat in the block next but one to ours.

They're home early in the morning and don't work in a hospital.
I go to the general store practising the phrase you've taught me
Under my breath. The first widower is there

With Martina who lifts her black muzzle to me and shows a pink tongue
Panting in what can only be described as pure happiness
As the second widower comes in to buy more rum

Whose even smaller dog practises his base notes on the girls
Who are dressed, not in mini-skirts, high heels and little else
But track suits. They practise their English on me.

They practise English greetings and will practise English farewells;
Good Afternoon, Good Afternoon, Good Afternoon, huskily rolling the r's
A sound like moths whirring on lampshades; *Good Afterrrnoon*.

They never get up in time to practise *Good Morning*,
But they practise what they can in front of racks with bottles of rum,
Cartons of cigarettes, rows of fish hooks

In packets of three, each with a brassy barb and a feather,
Pink, green and blue. *Good Afternoon, Good Afternoon, Goodbye*
As I forget that phrase for condolences.

Storks Returning

For Viera

All at once a long, silent procession of ideas,
Five hundred or more above the hills
Against an indefinitely coloured sky
Suave as porcelain, the birds black against the light.

The flock is a sprawling cuneiform
An archaic sentence that will not parse
Or a tuning fork with one tang broken off.
Strike it against the sky and you'd hear the creak of wings.

Languidly this writing loses shape, the birds
Hesitating over where they might have been last year.
Symbols begin to drop away from text,
Prehistory returning with its patient appetites.

I'd like two vases made, both with a glaze
Of grey suggesting cloud suggesting rain;
One for September with the flock painted there
Stretching their wings up to the vessel's rim, each bird's poise

Indicating a common destiny and I'd fill it
With gaudy, symmetrical, orange Chinese lanterns.
The second would be for this day in late March
With the flock scattering, birds spiralling down

Out of formation to their own purposes,
To empty villages whose good fortune is long used up.
In a month or so I'll fill it with the irregular
Indigos and whites of Siberian irises.

Thirty Storks and a Red Tin Box

Beyond a town where English has only lately come to roost
I shove a lawnmower across a rough and rooted place
Beside a foreign-talking brook, rowan, birch and spruce.

Behind my progress stems of plantain like tiny minarets
Survive, brown flowerheads intact, to disseminate
A thousand uprisings of seed in my empire of cut grass.

I wipe my loyal machine with octavos of dock and quit
My paradise of cabin, nightmare of a lawn and roseroot,
Wild garlic, golden rod, chicory, late cranesbill,

Colours of silences among the tree and water voices.
There's no one on the road until the forest diminishes to hazel;
Then an old man with a red tin box, the legend PASCAL

Painted on it in white lettering; then a field newly ploughed,
The turned clay folds of an umber quilt much rumpled
Over which thirty or more storks pick their way, finical

Yet voracious for frogs and mice exposed, displayed
To their enormous stare. They pause, they stoop, they gobble.
Cautiously I stop my car, walk among them, am ignored

By figures in nunnish black and white, legs and necks in slowed
Imitation of supermodel strut along a catwalk.
Part of me is earthbound, part wishes to join the flock

Stretching out in a line of flight to the Red Sea and the Nile
While part of me goes back to my car, scrapes my shoes with a stick,
Thinks of an old man and a red tin box with the legend PASCAL.

Chinoiserie

After a poem by Roy Fuller (1912–1990)

Grey-backed flycatchers scuttle up the hornbeam's trunk.
A redstart flies in under the veranda roof
And spreads and flutters its rusty tail uncertainly.
It has a rusty song, too, like the winch's chain
Creaking as a bucket descends into the well.

A bee alights upon the blotted manuscript
Of what I fancy is an important poem.
The sun has clouded over, the air cooled. So it rests
Between nectar source and hive. I withdraw my pen
And watch the quivering abdomen, the bristled

Thorax and chitinous head shaped like a broad nib
I might use for a painstaking calligraphy.
Bees rub their heads with their forelegs just like household cats.
In front of me is a bed of Chinese lanterns
Whose white flowers of effacement have opened out

Over seed pods dangling on stalks from leaf axils,
Vegetable still, green, veined, enclosing a smooth
Marbly seed. Behind them wasps hover above then grip
The round flowerheads of angelica. Bees moor
Themselves to burdock, but yarrow is left alone.

In Chinese verses a moral might be teased out
About how the rejected art of penmanship
Withers to stalks which can be used in divination
Falling this way or that, as Chinese poets did
In their cups, according to the will of heaven.

Alas, in this here and now poets simply age
And lose their powers of speech. Few of them garden.
None will imitate Po-chu-i, 'On Being Sixty',
Or make the yarrow plant sixth and seventh decades,
Twenty years of earned repose beyond the Five Lusts

Before the years of decrepitude prove tiresome
To dutiful sons and daughters. I'd try my hand
Were there not, hanging out linen on the balcony
Of the penzion above my cabin, a girl;
High-breasted, Tartar cheekbones and braids of copper.

So I think of my uncertain teeth, my white hair,
My wife's scorn; poetry the straight and narrow way
To encounter trouble. Just yards between girl and wife!
A bee-line between blonde and auburn flowerheads.
I should have praised the emperor's verse, stuck to prose.

Wild Strawberries and Gladioli

Wild strawberries hang in doubles of fruit,
Neither sweet nor sour, under toothed leaves
Beside purple self-heal and the hornbeam
Whose branches we pruned back earlier this year.
The sawn stumps wept a clear sap.

Wild strawberries! I could add them with advantage
To two full glasses of chilled champagne.
Yards away, it could be miles or years away,
You stand by gladioli, as tall as you,
Six-petalled, brassy gossips.

At night they'll shut up to papery twists.
You ask if you can cut some for your father's grave.
Horseflies raise welts on my shins and forearms
As I pluck wild strawberries – a favourite film
On time and memory,

Twin fruits, firm nipples the colour of blood,
And I offer you a handful of desire.
You turn your head aside when we kiss goodbye,
Taking to the dead the number custom here demands;
Four stalks with heads of flame.

Mayflies

i.m. James Merrill (1926–1995)

I sunbathe at the bottom of a well of green,
A thousand thousand tints; beech, acacia, pine
With its new growths of emerald buds, the linden
Whose scent is sharpest before storms, a birch tree's sheen
Or tinfoil glimmer in the breeze mayflies still rise upon.

Squinting, I look away from a stem's jade tip
To the vivid spider centred in a beer bottle top.
Rayed like a star it might sense a whole world in its grip.
It only has to wait and wait for something to drop
From what must seem to be nothingness as mayflies still rise up.

There's a warbler in the lindens whose stuttering cries
Are answered by another from the slope of beech trees.
A third also stakes a claim for territories.
I can't make any of them out so my gaze
Focuses on the space where mayflies still rise,

Miniature Chinese kites with split hairs for tail
Or the angels that dance on the end of a needle.
How many since morning have dizzied up from the pool?
How many hemi-demi-semi-quavers in a warbler's trill?
What else except death can make mayflies still?

Close to, my face must seem to them immense in size,
A wall of folds and sweat, monstrous grey-green eyes
Yet less eloquent with harm than the warbler's cries
Whose replies are questions and questions more replies
Unheeded by their prey which cannot hear: mayflies.

At Dusk

Forget-me-not on the bank of the brook,
Comfrey, bugle, yellow archangel,
A single flower of leopard's bane, chervil,
A dandelion gone to seed its stalk
Invisible in the dwindling light
So its spherical head seems to float
Above the grass like a tiny space station
And across the brook in the forest
The broad, simple leaves of honesty;
All this a mile downstream, fifty years on
From forced labour in an opal mine,
From the site of a Nazi atrocity.

At dusk three men scramble into our glade
And ask if we've seen a stray German Shepherd.
From their anger, their looks and rank breath I dub them
Dogbeater, Young Adolf and Nondescript Thug.
If we were in Kosovo I would be afraid.
The dog is drinking from the brook and is dragged
Back up the bank, but nips Dogbeater hard
And escapes again with all in hot pursuit.
You've hidden in our cabin away from brutes,
Away from their foul language and yelping dog.
Now you weep for loss of peace of mind.
The sun has set and a bird begins to sing.

It has perched on a fence I've built.
It lifts its left wing, then its right
Precisely to the horizontal.
It preens its flight feathers, trills to its mate.
No answer; so it repeats its signal
Raising its wings again like the indicators
Of a pre-war car, a Morris Minor
Or Volkswagen perhaps, a little dictator
When a wing twitches slightly higher
And a brief song is repeated – *Untrue,*
Untrue –. Untrue, I think, what we try to do.
Flowers still bloom, our massacres continue.

In the Country of Birds

A buzzard roosts by the highway
A glum functionary in the parliament of birds
Waiting to raise points of order or prey
Upon a careless puss-in-boots with a gold ring on its tail.

All this happens as storks return unseen
With their human-coloured legs, intelligent eyes
And beaks like the weapons of the scissor men
Who waited in Mother's wardrobe when we went to try her shoes on.

Later there are remote flurries of swallows like poppy seed
Flung against the sky and falling in slow motion,
The nightingale's imitation of everything he's heard,
A collective panic of starlings in the school yard.

Grandmother says it was when cottages stood on magpie legs:
Grandfather dressed a Jewish doctor and his wife
In peasant costume and sent them out with the hogs
To help potato pickers as the Gestapo hunted high and low.

Grandfather hid their jewellery in his house
Until the war was over. One gold ring was lost and a friend.
Perhaps the ring was juggled through a hole by a mouse,
Perhaps a cat ate up the mouse and wore a gold ring on its tail.

A bell ting-tangs from an onion dome
Made of wood and slate. The pungent notes that chime
Summon us to recite our perpetual fall from grace
And a promise of perfection with candle, book and hymn.

I will open a volume of light and shadow
Where two streams meet. When I turn the pages I will go
Up through the forest to where trees thin to rowan and juniper,
Where holy writ is left behind with the jay's bravado.

There in the grass I might find a nest of lark's eggs.
The bird will soar through fear not joy; its song diverts
Come away! Come away! And so I will, just like an ogre,
Rain clouds on my shoulders, striding over hills in seven league boots.

Ring Snake

Servatz, Pancratz and Bonifatz:
A cold north wind that breathes down our necks from the Pole
And the Middle Ages; not a gale
But a steadiness blowing from the Baltic across the Beskids
To where wild strawberries have spread
Their flowers like appliqué round the buttonholes
Beneath our daughter's layers of veil
Covering her first Communion dress. In places petals have been shed
For a scattering of drops of blood.

Not exactly sweet but tangy
As I stoop to pick and taste pausing from my task with a log.
I brush the earth away and drag it
To where I can stand it on its end and strip it of rotting bark.
It becomes a wooden tower, blonde, stark
From which a maggot waves like the white arm of Rapunzel.
I rub it down and lay it on the gravel
So we can sit close to the fire and forget about the cold
Huddled like children to whom a tale is told.

There's a ring snake on a bare stone
Like the mark left by the bottom of a dirty pot,
Yellow flashes on its head, fat
As though it has just fed, black tongue a flame of anti-matter
Scorching a route over the textures
Of clay, stick, strawberry leaves as I follow it
Towards the stream (though you do not)
Until it insinuates itself between ripple and rock
Vanishing to become water not snake.

What is it like to be a snake,
The whole world drumming into one's skin, touch and smell, touch and
smell?
To be held in a human hand must be hell
For a snake, that sudden heat, the palpitation of the little veins
In palm and finger. Much cooler the pains
To be taken among rock, soil, root, the delicate odour
Of prey; the egg of a warbler.
You've seen snakes play in water seeming to braid and unbraid
About one another. You were not afraid.

Servatz, Pancratz and Bonifatz:
Three western saints somehow drifting north to become this icy draught
Which will leave white frost upon the grass.
We watch a spider shuffle unseen cards between tree and tree
Suspended by other invisibilities
While our daughter comes to us in crisp new T-shirt, jeans and trainers.
Not the slightest speck of earth must stain her.
Cautious, elaborate, serpentine is the route she takes
Over strawberry leaves and the tracks of snakes.

March Adder

They say that one June fifty years ago
A goatherd swallowed an adder as he slept.
Villagers hung him upside down from a pear tree
And a saucer of warm milk was placed beneath his head.

The goatherd had to tell his story over and over.
No one noticed what happened to the snake
After it had dropped from his quaking throat into milk.
Whether it drowned or drank its fill, they do not say.

It's not June here but March and a young zig-zag
In printed violet skin has sidled out
From roots and mould beside a chinking, melting brook
Drawn forth by unseasonable milk-warm light.

My wife and daughter have skedaddled up the hill.
I hear their *Come away! For God's sake, come away!*
But take no notice as I stoop to watch more clearly
Its meander between bank of snow and bank of snow.

I hang my head delightedly above the snake.
I wish it well. I wish it dry space under twigs
Before the cold sets in again. I wish it
Not milk but an early fallen sparrow's egg.

Two Rattlesnakes in a Zoo

Here are two rattlesnakes
So looped about themselves
They can't be told apart.
Their heads rest side by side.
They could be joined at the neck,
A double beast, half dozing
As the other half explores.

A tongue of deep maroon
Dawdles over stones,
Itself, the other's scales
Or its double nature.
One tail end is visible;
The bony little finger
Of a withered saint.

In Cranach's painting
A full-fleshed smiling creature
Coils a green tail round a tree.
Rosy fingers grip a branch.
The other hand extends
A yellow apple. Words fall
From an undivided tongue.

It whispers the fruit is good.
The broken man, the woman
Severed from him eat, betray:
She gave to me to taste,
The serpent tempted me.
So a triple-natured voice,
Neither man nor woman, hisses
On thy belly thou must go.

In the garden we have made
Secure for threatened species
Two rattlesnakes are graceful;
One maybe fast asleep,
The other's vivid tongue
Sauntering over gravel,
Grains of sand, an iron grille.

It tastes the glass through which
Upright animals gaze.
Sometimes there is food,
Sometimes not. It slides on.
Dry-coloured eyes turn away
Above a silent mouth
Closed upon a punishment

For heels which bruise its head,
Bruises to be returned;
First red, then mauve, then black
Extending to the heart
And words of trust which stop
As innocence once stopped.
It cannot be revived.

The Light in the Elderberry

It's impossible to put into words, into sound,
The light in the elderberry
From the midday sun in February,
In the wild hair of twigs tangling from central shoots
Down to chunks of unmelted snow
Among logs left to decay.

Above us is a sky so blue it must be the ultimate
In the scattering of light.
And we crane our necks as if about
To see all the way through to deep space and star shine.
Just photograph the light
Says my serious Russian friend.

And so I focus on the hard glints and knife blade sheen
In snow and elderberry buds.
Below us the Malá Del'na thuds,
Whose groan can be heard soft or loud from the ravine
According to weather or season
Ten feet from our cabin.

When we go back I'll take shots of its sinuous water,
A cold muscle which flows
Between the remnants of the snows
Around the cabin and I'll put the prints with one I took
In Libya twenty years ago
Of fresh steak on a butcher's hook.

Nearby bullock heads had been piled into an old dustbin lorry
Painted in the corporation green
Of nineteen-fifties Britain.
Long lashed Black Angus eyes stared as if they still had sight.
Just photograph the light
Said my serious Russian friend.

Prickly Pears and Oranges

Prickly pears are a rabble of headless men
Whose limbs have yellow flowers drooping
Like cotton gloves with empty fingers.

Their fruit first appears livid as a rash
Then matures in carbuncular clusters.
Harvested they are pruned back to thickets

High and close enough to deter small boys
From banditry in the formal orange groves
Where young goats play king-of-the-castle.

Hacked, burnt, then ploughed in deep by claimants
To a promised land they resurrect
In a straggle of spiky ovals.

They reassert boundaries of alfalfa,
Of villages deliberately de-named,
Settled over, portioned in another tongue.

Rooted out again they still spring up
From the hidden stubbornness of seed,
A vegetable remembrance

Long after incinerated title deeds,
Long after the requisition document
Whose lie is 'for reasons of security',

Long after the exodus of smallholders;
Bemused old men on donkeys dreaming,
As they rode away, of prickly pears

And oranges – circles of ripeness,
Globes of paradise beneath glossy leaves –
Which could be quartered easily

For the satisfaction of the palate.
Now the memory of their taste provides
Bitterness for the politics of loss.

It is difficult to eat the prickly pear.
You have to soak it overnight
Otherwise the brittle spines break off

Then splinter as they lodge beneath your skin.
But if you manage to survive you open
A sweetness whose softened rind parts at your touch.

The Fossil

'If necessary we can go back to the desert'
(Reported of King Faisal during the oil crisis of 1974)

As is the custom we have perched
On thorn bushes a slim haunch
Of mutton and the rice we cannot eat,
Clear of the ground so only birds may feed.

Now under an acacia we sip tea
And watch dust devils skedaddle
Along the highway's grainy liquorice
Between a frail, odd expanse of seedlings.

Here iron giraffes clatter and lean down.
Their unimaginable mouths drink
From levels hundreds of feet beneath
As tankers, their round calves, suck water from them.

Sayer Al Harthy offers me a cigarette.
His robe's linen whispers with the gesture
Like paper tissue drawn from a box.
He has shown me the omega shape

Of stones which form a Bedu mosque
And explained with so few words that I think
Not even enormous wealth can drown
Habits made by economies of thirst.

He points to the fossil I have found,
A bean-sized snail or nautilus
Stone-dry for millennia, and asks
Teacher, tell me, where does this thing come from?

Out of courtesy or cowardice
I answer *From the time of dinosaurs*
And Noah when men prayed to animals
So that God covered the earth with water.

A Snail in Istanbul

The sultan of moisture creeps
On a flagstone shadowed by nettles.
He carries his turban on his back
And shows his tentacles, a scholar
Bareheaded out of the mosque.
No doubt his hidden mouth is prim
Though his tongue, rough with hunger
Not prayer, will rasp on greenery:
One foot, one lung, one kidney,
One gonad, mostly male, feminine
Only in summer in a place
The Turkish guidebook labels
The Convent of the Whirling Dervishes.

In the octagon of the dance hall,
On a balcony wall overlooking
The dancing floor is a photograph
Of abandoned holy men, a cluster
Of white frowns with unkempt beards
Like snails stuck to a glossy leaf.
They lingered after Sheikh Galib
The last, great formal poet,
Years after Halit Efendi
Whose body is in a tomb outside.
His head is buried elsewhere.
Their pens and mechanical verses
Are displayed, nibbled by neglect.

On the path the devotee of stealth
Has almost reached the nettles.
His spiral of shell and viscera,
His delicacy, will not be scourged
By the stinging hairs on the stems.
Far above him the curator
Picks tobacco from a lower lip
Before he brushes down the graves
Tilted by subsidence so they seem
Almost imperceptibly to make
A gesture in the dance. Their headstones
Are grey, bearded with inscriptions,
Crested with marble turbans.

Sunflowers

The fields are massed congregations of the faithful
With absurd collars on the thick necks of the truly stupid
Over the course of the day turning a callisthenic half-circle
Beneath an ever unbelieving green, slopes of pine and fir.

Close to an individual bloom it is as if my lack of regard
Was sustained at a great height from an aircraft
Over a black-roofed city with parallel boulevards
Curving to a centre without a statue of the founder.

Or perhaps I look without understanding at the coil
Of a slender rosary wound round a point slightly off centre
Which cannot be revealed to the sceptical
Who see only a mania for absolute order.

Within the yellow petals black singularities ripen
And haul bloom, haul yellowness, haul light into them.
Black is pure devotion, black is the husk round the oil of salvation,
Black is the fruit turned away from the sun, bowed to the earth.

Sometimes in October I see solitary sunflowers
In a field of thistles withered into rags, into protein,
Mortified desert fathers or stooping wilderness sisters
Righteous enough to receive their due reward from the birds of the air.

Otherwise the black flowerheads have been stripped of their vestments
And have gone to the devils of pet food or cooking oil
Or to salt and fire and teeth and lips of sentiments
Of those who spit the shells out between small talk and sips of vodka.

Magnolia

In this quiet before the storm I can almost hear the magnolias bloom,
The buds unsheathing in their bracts
To a mass of flamingo heads pointing at a hazy moon

While the street lamp's beam makes the cherry tree's gnarled growing
                                                              points
Seem webs of branch and twig on which
A raised white stitching means they'll bend soon in lazy, decorous do's
                                                         and don'ts.

Behind the trees lightning tears the night as though it were carbon paper,
Flimsiness ripped by sheer heat,
Blossoms of a million volts over what is right and proper.

You flinch at thunder, at apocalypse, you say God's Will Be Done.
In the morning on the river bank
Police will find a man dead from spring lightning or winter rum.

'It's miles away. We're safe here,' my comfort eddies to glibness
Or patters like the fat drops of rain
As I talk on about the magnolia exhibiting its flawless

Pinks and creams for a week then shedding all to leave armoured fingers,
Green at first and then vermilion
A process of water, nitrogen, hydrocyanins for colours.

We approach the street lamp's beam flawed with the drift and mottle of
                                                        a shower
Our shadows withering into themselves.
I lift my gnarled hands to the light and I watch my fingers flower.

The White Crow

What should we really make
of an idea of crows
flocking down from this oddly
peach-coloured winter evening?
They roost in the tops of trees
like unpicked fruit none could eat
or perch there, a denser kind
of mistletoe, pestilence
which has stripped each branch of leaf
instead of the season's cold.

Certainly the noise they make
is affliction, unsettling
for us as they stretch, settle
untidily, now shapeless
like shreds of a backcloth from
a theatre of the mind.
Their sound populates the air
with invective, drowning out
even a long train jangling
north to the Polish border.

I saw an albino crow
once at the railway station,
the wind icing from the north.
I was shivering and he,
I am assuming he, was
a put-upon gentleman
engaging me, the only
other living creature there
that late morning, in discourse;
I guess about the weather

or times which are always bad.
His squawkings, his mutterings,
his puckerings of sound grew
more and more perfunctory
as though he slowly came to
understand that I could not
understand his crow language.
He was a philosopher
probably of the matter-
of-fact, this red-eyed, ashen

dishevelled soul who might well
have been saying *I'll tell you
the rules of life. Paper covers
stone and stone blunts scissors and
scissors cut paper. That's all.*
Not a representative
of a cooing choir in white,
no angel, revelation,
but an aside as a train
jolted south to Hungary.

A Piece of Wood

For David Cobey

I find it as I would a phrase
I hadn't heard before; a sawn piece
Of twelve by two lying on the porch,
Flecked with dew, freckled where a wood wasp
Might have drilled, but now sterile, seasoned wood
Entire and clear as a cloudless sky,
Ready to be fitted into a house.
It's like a part of speech, unnoticeable
As the grammar we use to make of ourselves
A sounding box when speech rises through us,
And when we do not name ourselves but are named;
Birth or death with words spoken over us.

Is it a death to become not what we are,
Reliquary as driftwood, hacked and pitted
To the appearance of a stone
Which we stoop to examine and lift
Amazed at finding it so light,
Or else jostled in a line of surf
So it moves like antlers in a thicket?
Sometimes we find driftwood on a beach
Complete and simple as thighbones from a bull
Empty of marrow, daubed with oil,
And we heap it to blaze while night
Flourishes around us like a forest.

I know a lack of wood where such trees
As can thrive on drought deny themselves –
Cypress, a spiral of flaking greenstone,
Eucalyptus, supple as a solder.
There the horizons waver through outlines
Of thornbush, maimed fingers of cacti.
There the orange box is cherished
And if the imported measures
Of building timber are neglected
Moisture is sucked out and they bleach, split.
Wealth is a plump hand resting on polished
Mahogany, cedar, walnut and pine.

And survival is sifted as smoke
From charcoal where red tea coughs on a grill;
Smoke which is more visible
The further it circles from me
Not as particles of ash
But thickening like the branches
Of the olive tree it once was,
Now the signal of slow heat
Provider of the scent of households
Then spreading from cutting, graft or pip
To nourishment, oil glimmers,
A hardiness of love I've never found.

I fear an abundance of wood
As in rain forests whose creepers bind
Hardwood to softwood, the sapling
To the riddled trunk whose roots have crumbled.
My feet trample wafers of bark,
Soft chunks of sustenance for insects, seeds.
In such confusion I am afraid
To touch, to disturb, unlike a carver
Who is confronted only by heartwood,
Innocent stripped substance which undergoes
Impulse as his fingertips alight
On a little knot on the surface.

He strokes the blemish in the grain
As a lover might a nipple
Then slides his touch along letting the wood
Ripple beneath his skin finding
A form implicit for knife and chisel.
How much does he recall of the games
Which took us beyond the tyre iron
Suspended from an elm to make a swing
Out over a drop where children's cries
Fall safely into cut grass and moss?
How much does he recall of when we ran
Past initials scratched in bark,

Past firs meshing their branches to darkness,
Over their soft needle answers to footfall
And reached the sawmill where air was hazy,
Where the wood was torn and made ready?
A piece of it lies before me now,
A length of sawn twelve by two, flecked with dew,
Freckled with holes left by a wood wasp
But sterile now, no home for maggots,
Entire and clear as a cloudless sky,
Structured, to be fitted onto a porch,
To be unnoticeable as habit,
To be weathered, to be replaced at last.

Ferns

Within the permanent stink of creosote,
Next to conversation about engines,
Beside crates of Coca-Cola and rotting timber
The lady of the house grows ferns –
In her backyard, in saucepans, in glass jars
Which she stores upon the shelf above my head.

Sunshine through them makes a green batik
On the counterpane as I examine
A wrestle of stems in water
And touch rows of spores like microdots,
A secret message of propagation.

Yesterday we clambered a volcano's slope
Collecting ferns. We left the trees and grass
To find ourselves among smooth, green columns,
A Roman city now vegetable
Where tarantula and scorpion crouch.

We left our samples at the crater's edge
Before we scrambled down, hand over hand,
Through roots and slime to the sulphur springs.
Only one kind of fern could grow
Near that bubbling earth; something like an ear
On a single stalk, attuned perhaps

To the volcano's last gasp of origin
Or else the first hiss of an end to come.

Beyond

The sea heaves in slow motion as though composed
Of something denser than its true element.
I bait hooks and jerk in handlines
On which pink fish hang limp as rag.
Their dorsal fins are needles springing up
Like flick knives to lance a thumb.
Round here they are called *Welshmen*.

My born-and-bred island friend is whey-faced
And requests that we put in.
So we pitch and roll to the magnetic bay
Whose bedrock is a rumoured iron ore.
When we paddle in the lilac shallows
And wind out lines for dogfish, there is rain.
If history were sensuous it would feel

Like this, a warmth and moisture
Brushing the mind's skin, then forgotten.
On this island we can stumble
Over querns like bellies with deep navels,
Pick bone arrow tips or notice
Breaks in a cliff's sheer fall to the sea
Which were perching places for mass suicide.

But in this spot we are free of relic
And stretch and bathe at the end
Of a rainbow of events so unattached
To consequence that we might dwell
In a setting for pure fiction
Where waves slide irregular as paragraphs
In short stories with no twist in their tails.

Tropical Romance

A rusty birdscarer clinked
At the Atlantic villa.
But still a yellowbreast wheezed
From the bitter orange tree
As night fell and oil lamps were lit.

They were luminous goldfish
In their bowls of decorated glass
As the mad man softly told me how he'd seen
Globes of fire race along the channel
And how they might come calling for him.

Later with my sister's lipstick
He scrawled, *You won't poison me?*
On her dressing table mirror.
We sat up all night tormented
By mosquitoes as he tapped at her windows.

The morning after, the sea boomed like health
Behind the lawn and manjaneels
Whose caustic fruit is only food for crabs.
The older lovers with us strolled
Where huge caterpillars looped on twigs

Their happiness an emblem
For past and present. They must have thought,
We were once here as children and now look
What is happening to us!
While the future crept behind my sister

As she dived between the sloping waves.
I called to him. He turned around.
His eyes were blank and brilliant as if he gazed
To above the clouds where sky deepens
To a permanence of stars and comets.

Incident in Guatemala

Our tour was halted near a river
Whose water the washed-down clay had stained
To the colour of an abattoir.
Trees were snagged on the bridge's stanchions
And it was said that bodies from a killing
Had floated past a week before.

We were lined up and made to stand with arms
Stretched above our heads while our hands rested
On the flaking paintwork of the bus.
A border guard picked through our belongings
And another felt inside a blonde girl's blouse.
A third cocked a rifle, covering us.

We waited while the passport of ourselves
Was opened and stamped upon so we could go
Into a land of outrage beyond our sight
But audible as the girl cried out
And the guards made jokes. Across the border
I asked, uselessly, *Are you all right?*

But she did not answer. Instead she watched
Where light was glossy on plantation acres
Under a narcotic swish of rain
And where it glowed in the sheen of sweat
On arms which raised machete blades
And let them fall on dense, green sugar cane.

An Eisenhower Autumn in America

Unanswerable voices rise, pungent
as charcoal grilling steak for barbecues.
They gainsay his out-of-sorts, his dissent,
with sighs on how the maples burnish views

to gilded intervals between estates;
woods of the golden mean he motors through
past country clubs whose dressed stone moderates
love of profit with the proper virtue.

They praise achievement of the possible
each year in autumn. Even weather croons
with satisfaction as glimmers nibble
an edge of dusk fragrant as macaroons.

Could he claim obverse countries of desire
where pomegranates redden for the dead
and night snarls within haloes of white fire
converted by lightning to a wolf's head?

Of course not! He can't commit an error
of contrariness. This land's makers showed
a love of liberty not of terror.
So he recounts a journey on a road

stretched at first, like elastic, over downs
steep, gladed as landscapes by Fragonard;
then slackened to coil round slopes bare as Brown's
demure and treeless parks.
                                          Slowing my car

I turned off at my fairy grandma's home
which was wrapped for winter in polythene
altering the stone Montecello dome
to a tea cosy with a plastic sheen.

The low-paid help chopped wood upon a grate
covering the poisoned well, was puzzled
when the sticks slid through. A blue Ford coupé
rusted to its axles. Wind was muzzled

beneath the peeling planks' opaque sheeting.
By the porch late flowers bloomed in crisp white
like bonnets for Dutch dolls. Without greeting
she opened up and pulled me out of sight.

The whole first floor was given up to dogs.
Even a bath had become a seething
velvet of brown puppies. A stack of logs
hid an old German Shepherd whose breathing

wheezed down the stinking hall as she took me
to the kitchen, filled up a feeding bowl
with cold water, unhooked a leash, looked me
up and down, whispered that she'd have my soul

or disinherit. What else could I do?
When I knelt and tried to lap she secured
a studded collar round my neck. Then through
the muddy runs she tugged me while she toured

her kennels, my legacy. Near my car
she stooped, unclipped the leash, quickly arose
and said Goodbye or Good boy. The dog star
yelped. I drove off blindly, followed my nose.

For the Inauguration

'A savage servility slides by on grease'
(Robert Lowell)

You can't trust a man that cheats at basketball.
Sooner or later he comes along to say he'll lay down the law.
I'd like to lay down on the law; trousers or skirt
Makes little difference at my time of life. The sex maniac
I'm bound to slips his cuffs now and again so I'm free to speculate
      On all my might-have-beens.

I'll never attain that state of holy innocence
When I can be a frowning, private, naked man among schoolchildren
Telling them that the big, bad wolf is one of my friends
And is held to be a most trustworthy soul by the American Indian.
That's when the law steps in bouncing his ball on the fence
      Calling game over one point ahead.

He leads me away as I count how many letters in the alphabet
I've not come on to in a career wholly unpublicised
And not exposed to the scrutiny of a court:
Her Majesty the Queen definitely not, a Xenia I only taught.
Was there a U? There was a Wendy in a retreat
      Run by Ursuline nuns.

But I'm jolted out of my reverie by the law
Who wants to know about the bodies under the floor
He claims they're finding as they move his stuff in;
His exercise bike, his personal grins – his Me to You's.
'You mean my manuscripts?' 'Yes, we've seen the tattoos
      Inscribed on the deceased.'

Watermarked paper or spotty white skin, what's the difference?
I'd say I've left the world richer for people on balance.
Subtracting a minus is a plus and I've added to the alphabet,
Especially the A's and J's and M's and an overweight
Rounder letter, inking her beautiful circumference;
      O, O, O, O, that O!

Besides all of us walk on the bones of the dead,
Breathe in the idea of flesh in the words they once said
Or dribble and slam-dunk after the whistle's blown
Arguing that the game was not over, forgetting that the law
Can blow time whenever he chooses, when the score
        Looks fairly in his favour.

The world gets the Don Giovanni it deserves,
A reedy performance muffing his bass notes time after time
No better than the thunk of basketballs, the body swerves
Of the living, faking, tuneless athlete fighting what he calls crime.
I'm off. The flagstones in the piazza get on my nerves.
        No knowing what they hide;

Perhaps a stonier version of the law
His fingertips spinning a boulder meant for me.
There's an abandoned orchard needs my pruning saw.
Fruit trees with lichen on the north side of their trunks
Define how far I've come, my cells' built-in entropy
        With not a milkmaid in sight.

Afterwards a scythe, not motor mower, to clear the grass.
Shooting stars at night promise that nothing evil will come to pass.
Sooner or later, though, someone comes along to lay down the law
And bids me pick up an axe and be a good neighbour.
For there are country clubs to be built to order
        And, of course, money to be made.

Gee! I'd like to lay down good and proper on the law
And chop away at that regulation serge material.
But I can't pick up an axe or basketball
To cut the out-of-date down to size or to play to win.
Without the pleasure principle murder is a sin.
        I count my liver spots instead.

Sooner or later I'll pick up my voice and stammer
That the only body I've harmed is Standard English grammar,
But the law confirms my sentence for the twentieth of June.
Someone truly wicked will bounce a basketball on my headstone
And all America's TV will still have policemen, white in manner,
        Despite their lovely tinted skin.

Impersonal

It is not the human grease
Stored and isolated
Like unstable elements
In Egyptian Washington.

It is a disc of gristle
Ruptured in an accident.

It is not a dream of isotopes
Put into practice with love
And searchlights, made malleable,
Feminine, victimised.

It is the version of comfort
Imparted by morphine.

It is not the mouse I found
Slit open on the carpet
Whose heart I scooped from plush
With an edge of cardboard.

It is a scar from operations
Pressing on nerve tissue.

It is not the tar machine
At an opening in the wood
Nor the creeper I unpicked
From a concrete post.

It is the patient training
Of posture away from pain.

It is not the coloured climbing frame
For children. It is not where
Sycamore and maple chill
To saffron and maroon.

It is the denial of ease
Radiating in the next room
Where a woman exercises
Quietly for her life's sake.

Julie's Recovery

crying, crying and crying and crying
That everything was wrong. So they gave Julie
Something to drink and she dwindled to sighing

to sighing that everything was wrong. She would sit
On the edge of the bed with her legs apart
Like a man, so calmed she could not even spit

could not even spit out drugs which lulled meaning
And took away all her self-accusation.
She no longer had to insist on cleaning

on cleaning each careful answer of sense
With fingers which picked, picked at the thread
Of her mouth, at words which stuck at each tense

at each tense conversation until her lips
Only were alive and those fingers she rubbed
So often that callouses formed on their tips

on the tip of her tongue when she uttered again
Her fingers now folded as she stitched up the sounds
In patterns of knowledge made out of pain.

Out of pain she and mother walk in the zoo.
They stop to look at a young chimpanzee.
The animal shits and eats its way through

its way through the handful it keeps. Mother heaves
And covers her mouth with white Irish linen.
But Julie has seen worse so she turns and leaves

turns and leaves, not sickened, while Mother follows
Muttering, be *It cannot natural.*
I've read that a cage drives them but she swallows

she swallows *mad,* muffled in the handkerchief
With which she still dabs at her mouth unconsciously.
Julie regards her with a kind of relief

with a kind of relief feeling no urge
To complete Mother's sentence then snap back
So you think I'm insane! overcome by the surge

surge of words into screaming at each eyebrow
Raised in surprise. But now she says gently
Yes, I will always be ill. She can allow

allow Mother's excuse. For all threats are dying
As Julie strolls on, free not to care at all
Her thoughts flying and flying, flying, flying